Living God's Word

Practical Lessons for Applying Scripture to Life

Waylon B. Moore

Learning Activities and Leader Guide
by Jimmy Hester

LifeWay Press
Nashville, Tennessee

© Copyright 1997 • LifeWay Press
Reprinted 1999
All rights reserved

ISBN 0-7673-2604-0

Dewey Decimal Classification: 248.4
Subject Heading: CHRISTIAN LIFE

This book is the text for course CG-0224 in the subject area Ministry in the Christian Growth Study Plan.

Unless otherwise indicated, Scripture quotations are from the NEW AMERICAN STANDARD BIBLE.
© Copyright The Lockman Foundation, 1960, 1962, 1963, 1968,
1971, 1972, 1973, 1975, 1977, 1995
Used by permission.

Scripture quotations marked NIV are from the Holy Bible, *New International Version,*
copyright © 1973, 1978, 1984 by International Bible Society.

Scripture quotations marked Williams are from the *Williams New Testament,*
The New Testament in the Language of the People, by Charles B. Williams. Copyright © 1937, 1966, 1986
by Holman Bible Publishers. Used by permission.

Scripture quotations marked *The Message* are from *The Message.*
Copyright © 1993, 1994, 1995. Used by permission of NavPress Publishing Group.

Scripture quotation marked Knox is from *The Psalms: A New Translation* by Ronald Knox.
Copyright © Sheed and Ward, Inc., 1947.

Order additional copies of this book by writing to Customer Service Center, MSN 113;
127 Ninth Avenue, North; Nashville, TN 37234-0113; by calling toll free (800) 458-2772;
by faxing (615) 251-5933; by ordering online at *www.lifeway.com;* by emailing
customerservice@lifeway.com; or by visiting a LifeWay Christian Store.

For information about adult discipleship and family resources, training, and events,
visit our Web site at *www.lifeway.com/discipleplus.*

Printed in the United States of America

LifeWay Press
127 Ninth Avenue, North
Nashville, Tennessee 37234-0151

LifeWay.

As God works through us, we will help people and churches know Jesus Christ and seek His kingdom
by providing biblical solutions that spiritually transform individuals and cultures.

Contents

The Author

Waylon B. Moore has crisscrossed the United States and more than 70 countries to teach church leaders, seminary faculty, and hungry Christians how to mentor and disciple others to their maximal potential. In his interactive "Living God's Word" and "Mentoring Mandate" conferences Moore combines humorous stories, practical tools, and insightful principles from God's Word to bring a fresh approach to Scripture and lifestyle mentoring.

As a single adult, Moore was deeply concerned about the number of new believers who never grew. He began teaching principles of application in a variety of ministries. In Boston he mentored students at Harvard and MIT while on staff with the Navigators. Moore also worked in Billy Graham crusades in the United States and Europe.

Moore knows firsthand how to follow up new Christians and how to develop leaders. For 13 years he pastored a church in Tampa, Florida, that averaged one hundred baptisms annually and grew to three thousand members.

Moore's goal is to equip believers to evangelize, nurture, mentor, and multiply worldwide. For 11 years he was a guest lecturer to all new Southern Baptist missionaries, teaching methods of assimilation. He has written *New Testament Follow-Up, Multiplying Disciples,* the *Building Disciples* notebook, *First Steps,* and *The Power of a Mentor.* Parts of his books are in 26 languages.

Moore has degrees from Baylor University, Southwestern Baptist Theological Seminary, and LeTourneau University. Moore and his wife, Clemmie, have two grown children, Martha and Bruce, who serve in full-time ministry.

To contact Moore about speaking at your church or conference or to subscribe to the *Mentoring* newsletter, call the Missions Unlimited office at (813) 238-2303 or write to Missions Unlimited; P.O. Box 8203; Tampa, FL 33674-8203.

Week 1
Welcome to the Banquet

Day 1
Come to the Table

*I*magine an elegant dining table, set with the finest china and crystal. The doorbell rings. The guests are irresistibly drawn into the dining room by the aroma of the food. In awe, they comment on the festive occasion and on the impressive display of food.

Oddly, after an hour of observing the food, the company moves toward the front door, shaking hands with their hosts. "We so enjoyed it," they express with gratitude. The experience is over. The guests drive into the night, still hungry. No one ate.

This strange story of a rejected meal is duplicated in many churches on Sundays. People are there, perhaps week after week. They listen to the music and the sermon. Afterward they shake hands with the pastor-chef, saying, "I enjoyed the message." But many never "eat."

Over the past week which Scriptures from your Bible study, a sermon, or a lesson challenged you to repentance, renewal, or new habits? List one or two references below.

_____

_____

God invites us to a banquet of Scripture that is totally satisfying and fully adequate for every need in life. The apostle James exhorts us to "prove yourselves doers of the word, and not merely hearers who delude themselves" (Jas. 1:22). In other words, God doesn't say, "Just hear it!" He says, "Just do it!" What happens when you dare to apply the Bible? It can revolutionize the world. In the 16th century one verse sizzled in the heart of a quiet man. This monk was staggered when he came across this simple verse: "The righteous man shall live by faith" (Rom. 1:17). This phrase became the foundation of the Reformation begun by Martin Luther. Living God's Word means putting it to use for a practical purpose. When Luther put God's truth to use, he influenced nations. The Bible was translated into other languages so that common people who didn't read Hebrew, Greek, or Latin could understand it.

THIS WEEK'S LESSONS
Day 1: Come to the Table
Day 2: God's Word Satisfies
Day 3: A Healthy Appetite
Day 4: Digest Great Food
Day 5: You Are What You Eat

FOCUS
This week you will learn the value of assimilating Scripture into your life and will discover tools for applying God's truths.

MEMORY VERSE
*Thy words were found and I
    ate them,
And Thy words became for
    me a joy and the delight of
    my heart;
For I have been called by
    Thy name,
O Lord God of hosts
    (Jer. 15:16).*

What is the result of living the Scriptures? You get a new wardrobe as you follow the command to "put on the Lord Jesus Christ" (Rom. 13:14). Big changes occur! It's as if the Bible dresses in your clothes every day. People are "reading" God's Word through your life—as you walk and talk in your home, factory, business, or college classroom.

The Bible is like a supermarket. It empowers us with soul food—31,175 verses that are like canned goods and food packages to the hungry soul. The lessons in this book will give you "can openers" to open God's Word and to make it come alive.

The Bible: Inspired and Practical

Read 2 Timothy 3:15-17 in the margin. In this passage and others, Bible writers constantly affirm two major points about Scripture: (1) it is inspired, and (2) it changes and equips us.

From childhood you have known the sacred writings which are able to give you the wisdom that leads to salvation through faith which is in Christ Jesus. All Scripture is inspired by God and profitable for teaching, for reproof, for correction, for training in righteousness; that the man of God may be adequate, equipped for every good work (2 Tim. 3:15-17).

The word *Scripture* means *inspired writings.* And the word *inspired* means *God-breathed.* Scripture is from God's mouth and nostrils. The apostle Paul claimed four unique truths about this wonderful Book:

- Scripture gives wisdom that leads to salvation through faith in Christ.
- Scripture is all from God—"God-breathed."
- Scripture is dramatically profitable for living.
- Scripture equips and empowers you for every good work.

Not only is the Bible from God, but it is also for us. In 2 Timothy 3:16 Paul used the word *profitable* to describe this practical Book.

"All Scripture" is profitable. It is "living and active and sharper than any two-edged sword, and piercing" (Heb. 4:12). It is for now. You can take it home with you.

Verse 16 describes four "profitable" responses God has invested in His Word: teaching, reproof, correction, and training in righteousness. Every verse in the Bible has implanted in it at least one of these four ingredients to empower you to be like Christ. If you link each of these four nouns to a verb, you'll see the action! The Bible is profitable for—

- teaching—what I should know;
- reproof—what I should stop;
- correction—what I should change;
- training—what I should start doing.

Response to these actions speeds the process of your growth into Christlikeness. The Lord's power and abilities infuse you when you respond to His Word.

Know It

The first point you read about the Scripture's profitability is that it teaches you what you should know: doctrine. Only the Bible gives us the true and balanced view of life. You can have right doctrine and wrong living, but you can't have wrong doctrine and right living. As God's Spirit speaks through His Word, you'll begin to detect areas of compromise in your life. You will see yourself, people, and events from God's viewpoint, in related patterns instead of as curious accidents.

For instance, when you read a verse, ask yourself what doctrine it is teaching that you should know.

🍃 **Read 1 Peter 1:15 in the margin. What is the doctrine in the first part of this verse that we should know? Fill in the blanks.**

God is _____ and has _____ me to be like Him.

Like the Holy One who called you, be holy yourselves also in all your behavior (1 Pet. 1:15).

You may have identified that God is holy and has called you to be like Him. In addition, this doctrine may trigger a response: are you holy in all of your actions? God's Spirit may further prompt you to confess an ungodly attitude or action.

Stop It

The Bible is also a storehouse of reproof: what you should stop doing. Like a car horn, the clanging of a railroad crossing, and a red traffic light, God commands, "Don't do it." In a culture in which right and wrong are blended into "doing your own thing," the Scriptures warn you of impending danger. You hear a sermon or read a passage, and ding-ding-ding! Inside your heart echoes: "No longer. Put on the brakes now. Stop!"

How does the Bible say, "Stop"? Sometimes in the life of a Bible character, such as Samson or David, we read the tragic results of not heeding a stop signal. The consequences of running a red light are disastrous.

Sometimes God speaks a "Stop" with a principle: "Lead me in thy truth and teach me" (Ps. 25:5). You think, *Am I totally honest, truthful?* This means giving back the change the checkout clerk gave you by mistake. What you say must be transparent truth.

The Scriptures warn you of impending danger.

🍃 **Has God told you, "Don't do it!" recently? ❏ Yes ❏ No If so, what Scripture did God use to get your attention? Write it below.**

_____

_____

Change It

The Bible grabs our attention, causing us to correct our off-track direction. It's profitable not only for what we should know and stop but also for what we should change: "We all … are being transformed into [the Lord's] image from glory to glory" (2 Cor. 3:18). The first time I traveled across the Pacific Ocean, I was in a four-motor, former bomber-type airplane. We flew from Los Angeles to Guam—a tiny island, a speck in the giant Pacific Ocean. I asked the pilot how they would find it, since nothing was past Guam for hundreds of miles except a few green islands without landing strips. The pilot said, "Well, we've got three major things we use to hit our target." He discussed trigonometry, shooting the stars, and wind-drift angle. That didn't help me at all. I had flunked trigonometry twice in high school. When he told me that wind-drift angle meant that they pointed the plane not toward Guam but in a direction that allowed the wind to blow us toward Guam, I wanted to respond, "Let's pray!" But he continued, "We use these three interlocking resources to make constant, tiny changes in our direction to find the island perfectly." And we did.

Your life needs the constant, continual correction of the Word.

Your life also needs the constant, continual correction of the Word. The winds try to blow you off course. Strong winds blow—the influence of family background or friends' advice. Cultural winds hit you. Sometimes it's an attitude that needs changing, buried in the heart. Then God's Scripture-radar lovingly convicts you of the need to change your direction.

Perhaps the direction you're heading is OK and normal but is not God's desire. The Lord may want to upgrade your standards or your sensitivity to your spouse. A verse jumps out at you, announcing God's will: "I've got a better way! I give you the power to choose My best." One day Proverbs 13:10 popped up and "interrupted" my devotional reading: "Arrogant know-it-alls stir up discord, but wise men and women listen to each other's counsel" (*The Message*). Instantly I recalled a recent argument with my dear wife. I was convicted. My pride! I had to change. The verse has become my lifetime evaluator.

Start It

Finally, the Word is profitable for training in righteousness. This involves what you should start, or begin to do. God gives you a new plan, an insight to apply, a resolution to a problem. If you're in the Book, He gently directs, opening your life to what you should learn and know, what you must stop, where you need to change, and how you can start.

Before our church's revival meeting one year, I was preparing my heart in prayer. The Spirit of God reminded me of "Be devoted to one another in brotherly love" (Rom. 12:10). A forgotten disagreement came to mind. I had argued impatiently, quoting Scripture, with a friend about his battle with another church member. He had left our church, and I'd never called to mend things. So obediently but fearfully I drove to his house. I humbled myself and asked that he forgive my unloving attitude. He forgave me. I soared back home with a new start in my walk with God! And our church experienced God's fresh anointing. Living God's Word—it's sometimes frightening but never dull!

🌿 **Try this. Read Romans 13:8-14. Across a sheet of paper draw four columns. Label the columns *Know, Stop, Change, Start*. Reread the passage, looking for things God desires for you to know, stop, change, and start. Write a verse number and a brief description that applies to you. Circle one thing you will do this week to put that idea into practice.**

Every verse contains one or more of these four life-changing dynamics. Wherever you are—that's where the Spirit of God will use the Bible to meet you, "so that the man of God may be perfectly fit, thoroughly equipped for every good enterprise" (2 Tim. 3:17, Williams). Dig in.

Wherever you are—that's where the Spirit of God will use the Bible to meet you!

Day 2
God's Word Satisfies

*G*rowing up in the West, my brother and I played cowboys, "shooting" each other with homemade wooden guns. My Sunday School teacher, Mrs. H. C. Wallen, was a fabulous storyteller. Acting out the account of David and Goliath, she vividly described how David, the "Boy Scout of Israel," threw a straight rock and killed the savage giant. *What a guy! I want to be like David,* I thought.

The next day at school a bully punched my friend. In defense I threw a rock and hit him. When the kid screamed and fell, I felt triumphant, but there was no applause. Instead, a teacher escorted me to the principal. My tearful explanation didn't stop Mrs. Hilton from spanking me. She asserted, "You're not 'David' in this school." I was perplexed. David hit a bully and became king. I hit a bully and got spanked! *The Bible is for Sunday School, not grade school,* I decided.

Sadly, this crisis in relating practical spiritual truths to life is not limited to children. The Bible is often for show, like a pretty coffee-table book.

Why is God's Word used so little? One reason is that people see the Bible as an ancient book for a different civilization. Also, our Western mind-set tends to divide life into categories. An executive said to his friend that when he's at home, he leaves his business at the office, and when he goes to work, he leaves family and religion at home.[1]

Even prophets can lose the freshness of Scripture's speaking to their hearts. The prophet Jeremiah had been depressed because of the sins of his nation and its resulting exile in a foreign country. People rejected God's disturbing, unpopular message. Jeremiah discovered the secret of encouragement under pressure. The prophet recalled:

Thy words were found and I ate them,
And Thy words became for me a joy and the delight of my heart;
For I have been called by Thy name, O LORD God of hosts (Jer. 15:16).

Read Jeremiah 15:16 three times as you begin to memorize it this week. The verse above is quoted from the *New American Standard Bible*. You may memorize the verse from another translation if you wish.

Note the phrase "Thy words were found." Had God's message been lost or misplaced? It seems so. Having a stack of Bibles doesn't guarantee that God's Word won't be lost. The Bible can be lost in three surprising ways.

1. *Picking the wrong packages.* Have you ever seen a crying child in a food store screaming, "I want broccoli"? Kids want candy! Initially, most Christians have difficulty choosing the right bottle or package from the giant Bible supermarket. Which verses are best? Sadly, few baby believers have active spiritual parents to counsel them. Most flounder.

2. *Settling for substitutes.* Substitutes crowd out God's Word so that it gets lost. Satan packages colorful counterfeit food—sin—to attract the customer. The enemy short-circuits the Bible's power in our lives through " 'the worries of the world, and the deceitfulness of riches, and the desires for other things' " (Mark 4:19). Call them the security motive, the success motive, and the sex motive. Many believers substitute spoiled motives for the satisfying meat of obeying God (see John 4:34), and they die of starvation.

3. *Evading the unfamiliar.* A believer may reject nourishing food because he or she is not used to it. It's unfamiliar. My appetite has been turned off as I've seen french-fried grasshoppers sold on street corners in Bangkok and termites offered by smiling people in Zambia. In a similar way, many words and expressions are foreign to those reading the Bible for the first time.

You may be missing God's Word because you are picking the wrong packages, settling for substitutes, or evading the unfamiliar. Circle the number beside the one you will commit to eliminate in your Bible study. Pray for wisdom and strength to remove this barrier to your spiritual growth.

Substitutes can crowd out God's Word.

Application Changes Lives

The Scriptures aren't to be heard, read, memorized, or even acted out in isolation. That was the deadly disease Christ pointed out to the religious and disciplined Pharisees of His day. Application should naturally follow the study of God's Word. Tragically, it rarely does! God's Word, Jesus Christ, did not come to earth as paper and ink but as flesh and blood. Truth had legs!

Unlike a coffee-table book, the Bible is more like a cookbook in the hands of a novice cook. You go to it desperately, and the Word works, when put to use. Christians need a way to link God's power to both the triumphs and tragedies of their social lives, homes, and workplaces.

God's power is linked to your everyday life through your Teacher, the Holy Spirit. He may highlight a Scripture from a sermon, from your personal time with God, or from a Bible study. Then, like sticking together two matching strips of Velcro, the Holy Spirit attaches the meaning of a verse to a matching piece of your world.

"Don't fool yourself into thinking that you are a listener when you are anything but, letting the Word go in one ear and out the other. Act on what you hear! Those who hear and don't act are like those who glance in the mirror, walk away, and two minutes later have no idea who they are, what they look like" (Jas. 1:22-24, *The Message*). God's Word is a mirror, revealing spiritual blemishes and flaws.

> **Recall a recent experience when God's Spirit attached the meaning of a verse to a matching piece of your life. Write the reference and a brief description below. Share the verse with a friend as a testimony of God's work in your life.**

Reference: _____

Life application: _____

Thanking God in Problems

It took 13 years after that rock throw at Hubbard Elementary School before I saw the Bible graphically and rightly related to life. The experience was unforgettable. I was with five friends in an old Chevy. Suddenly, pow! Thump, thump! Brakes screamed as we carefully swerved and stopped with a blown-out tire. Our driver began to pray: "Thank You, Lord, for taking care of us. By faith we want to claim 1 Thessalonians 5:18: 'In every thing give thanks: for this is the will of God in Christ Jesus concerning you' [KJV]. We give You thanks in this circumstance. Please help us get a spare tire."

Did he hit his head? I wondered. I opened my eyes. *He must be crazy thanking God that way! We're stranded at 11:00 p.m., and we have no money!*

God's power is linked to your everyday life through your Teacher, the Holy Spirit.

Three guys with faith volunteered to look for a tire replacement. I stayed with the car. About an hour later the fellows returned and excitedly told this story. Rolling the bad tire down the road, my friends saw the lights of a service station blocks away. When they arrived, they explained our dilemma. The man replied, "I've got a used tire or a new one cheap." Sheepishly the guys replied: "We don't have money for a new or a used one. Could we look for a matching tire and exchange ours for a slick one in that pile you're selling for retread?"

The man grudgingly said, "Go look." They found a slick replacement tire, and the man helped them put it on the wheel. Thanking the man, my friends boldly shared their faith and soon led the service-station owner to Christ.

After hearing this story, I was convicted of my unbelief. This was the first time I'd seen a friend my age apply a verse in the middle of a problem! He claimed 1 Thessalonians 5:18 about the blown tire. That the Bible worked now, that God would travel out of His universe into my little frame of life—these were revolutionary thoughts, exploding in my heart and mind.

> **What did God say to you during today's study? Review and underline the statement that was most significant for you.**

> **Try to write this week's memory verse in the margin.**

> **Close today's lesson with prayer. Thank God for His Word and for the joy and delight it brings to your life.**

---

[1]As quoted by Joseph M. Cross, "Historical and Contemporary Trends in Biblical Application" (master's thesis, Dallas Theological Seminary, 1985), 3.

Day 3
A Healthy Appetite

*H*ow do you develop a healthy appetite for God's Word? You come to God with a seeking heart: "Taste and see that the Lord is good" (Ps. 34:8). Look at some of the precious promises God makes to those who are truly hungry:

"Blessed are those who hunger and thirst for righteousness, for they shall be satisfied" (Matt. 5:6).

That the Bible worked now, that God would travel out of His universe into my little frame of life—these were revolutionary thoughts, exploding in my heart and mind.

I will pour water upon him that is thirsty, and floods upon the dry ground (Isa. 44:3, KJV).

He has satisfied the thirsty soul,
And the hungry soul He has filled with what is good (Ps. 107:9).

Wouldn't you like a fresh sense of fullness from the Lord today? What do we possess that God feels is valuable enough to release the treasures of His heart? One thing. God answers in both the Old and New Testaments: a thirsty soul!

Jesus cried out, saying, "If any man is thirsty, let him come to Me and drink. He who believes in Me, as the Scripture said, 'From his innermost being shall flow rivers of living water' " (John 7:37-38).

Every one who thirsts, come to the waters;
And you who have no money come, buy and eat.
Come, buy wine and milk
Without money and without cost (Isa. 55:1).

It's sobering to say, "You have just as much of God as you want." Really! Anyone who comes thirsty and hungry to Christ can become spiritually rich beyond measure.

"Come to Me" is Jesus' simple invitation and three-word summary of the Bible (see Matt. 11:28). John echoed his Master's call: "The Spirit and the bride say, 'Come.' And let the one who hears say, 'Come.' And let the one who is thirsty come; let the one who wishes take the water of life without cost" (Rev. 22:17). And the Old Testament prophets sing the same transcendent melody across the centuries: God is seeking you; come to Him freely.

Anyone who comes thirsty and hungry to Christ can become spiritually rich beyond measure.

Develop an Appetite

Nothing promotes our thirst and hunger for God more than a daily time in the Word and prayer. Expose your heart to Him in daily devotional times. Ask the Lord to make you hungry for a deeper relationship with Him. For years I had not realized that getting saved meant that I had a personal relationship with God: "God has sent forth the Spirit of His Son into our hearts" (Gal. 4:6). Jesus lives in me—literally (see Gal. 2:20). Having Jesus Christ means having everything you need. All of the true treasures—the treasures of wisdom and knowledge—are wrapped up in the person of Christ (see Col. 2:3).

Besides spending personal time with God daily, be open to learn from people who model the application of Scripture. You'll learn rapidly this way. You can see a truth modeled in others and can then incorporate the principle into your life.

God speaks through diverse experiences, many people, and even simple circumstances.

Always keep one eye on the Word as you look to others who follow Christ. God speaks through diverse experiences, many people, and even simple circumstances. Some of God's supreme stimulators to application have been my wife and children. I also have gracious friends I've discipled who exhort me about a blind spot in my life, a bad attitude, or a sin (see Heb. 3:13).

God also fuels my thirst when I read Christian biography. When you read biographies of persons who have walked well with God, you enter their time in history and their thoughts. You learn from their mistakes, their faith, and their challenges. You draw courage to press on in the face of your own skirmishes by reading about their battles and triumphs.[1]

Of the three suggestions offered, which one do you need to focus on, beginning today, in your spiritual growth? Check one.
❑ **Having a daily time with God**
❑ **Learning God's direction through other people**
❑ **Reading Christian biography**

Write one action you will take this week to develop a healthy appetite for God's Word.

_____

Decide to Eat

What happens next? The next step is making the decision to eat: "Thy words were found, and I ate them" (Jer. 15:16). Jeremiah expressed the determination of a man who took to heart what God said. The Holy Spirit seems to categorize Scripture into two levels of food.

First, God nourishes you in the basics. Baby food is for those without spiritual teeth. The apostle Peter exhorts, "Like newborn babes, long for the pure milk of the word, that by it you may grow" (1 Pet. 2:2). Milk is the perfect food source for a while. To miss the basics is to miss the building blocks of spiritual power for your life. Too often new converts are not helped to absorb the nutrition that produces strong spiritual bones and muscles. What are some critical baby-food doctrines and habits that grow babes in Christ into mature disciples?

- Identification with Christ and His will in believer's baptism
- Daily intake of Scripture and a time of prayer
- Regular, close fellowship with an accountability group of mature believers
- A method of witnessing and a vision for the lost
- A steady diet of the Gospels to develop a love for Jesus Christ, with a focus on the Epistles to learn practical living

What would you add to the previous list of basics?

_____

_____

The purpose of mother's milk, formula, and strained carrots is to eventually prepare the baby for solid food. Baby-food doctrine is essential but not enough for mature growth into Christlikeness. To win in the race of life, you also need the long-range energy that comes from the meat of Scripture. We are able to eat meat after receiving the nourishment of milk and developing spiritual teeth to bite into the tougher teachings of God's Word.

The writer to the Hebrews addressed immature believers who hadn't developed the teeth to chew the meat of Scripture: "Everyone who partakes only of milk is not accustomed to the word of righteousness, for he is a babe. But solid food is for the mature, who because of practice have their senses trained to discern good and evil. Therefore leaving the elementary teaching about the Christ, let us press on to maturity" (Heb. 5:13—6:1). Without the nourishment of God's Word, a believer becomes spiritually malnourished, and growth is retarded. My son Paul was born with a condition known as tuberous sclerosis. A Diphtheria-Pertussis-Tetanus vaccination when he was six months old caused a further reaction in Paul's body, resulting in brain damage. Paul was mentally handicapped to a degree that he couldn't add two plus two. Outwardly, though, he grew to be six-feet-four.

Haven't you seen the same type of Christians? Their spiritual handicaps might not show up until you get to know them. On the outside they are six-feet-four-inch Christians. Inwardly, though, they're spiritually disabled.

God's heart aches for those who have great potential but who stay at the baby stage. "Come to Me," Jesus beckons. You'll gain and maintain a desire to apply God's Word if you cultivate a healthy appetite for it.

> To win in the race of life, you need the long-range energy that comes from the meat of Scripture.

What are you eating spiritually these days? Where are you on the following continuum? Mark your stage with an *X*.

Milk   Meat

Pray that the Lord will increase your hunger for His Word. Commit to move beyond milk to meat as you mature in your spiritual life. Write your prayer on the next page.

_____

_____

_____

_____

Day 4
Digest Great Food

The human body, when healthy, instinctively consumes and absorbs food. But whether you've been a Christian for five weeks or 50 years, you don't instinctively digest the Word. The how-to part of this process involves answering three vital questions:

- What does the passage say?
- Why was the passage written?
- How am I to experience the passage now?

What Does the Passage Say?

Ask the Holy Spirit for wisdom to discover what God is saying. Observe the passage carefully. Visualize what you read. Read again and again the passage or verse. Read it slowly, thoughtfully, with attention, with surprise, with care. What does it really say? Think. Find a quiet place where you can hear God speak to you. If you get tired, read standing up. Read passionately. Try reading the passage aloud to God. This is a simple but powerful way to focus on what the verse says. Many miss the actual meaning of a verse or passage with their rush to get through.

Let's work through a verse as we learn the process of digesting the Word. Read Matthew 7:7 in the margin. Now read it again carefully, using the methods described above. What does it say?

_____

_____

"Ask, and it shall be given to you; seek, and you shall find; knock, and it shall be opened to you" (Matt. 7:7).

Why Was the Passage Written?

Discover the historical setting of the passage. Get under the skin of the author—his people group, place, and period in history. Ask: To whom was this passage written, when, and why? What question is the author answering that was asked by those people long ago?[1] Perhaps you'll want to read an introduction to that book in your Bible or a commentary. At times the passage contains instruction for a particular culture; however, beneath it is a principle echoed elsewhere in Scripture that is also for you now.

The human writers were not robots. Some writers had great education, while others used everyday speech. Yet the God who made, numbered, and named the stars (see Ps. 147:4) ensured that the Scriptures never err in the truths they proclaim and explain.

"What if I get it wrong because I know so little about the Bible?" you may ask. Come to the Lord with a hungry and pure heart. God meant for His Word to be understood by everyone, not just by a select minority. Pray what David prayed:

Break open your words, let the light shine out,
let ordinary people see the meaning (Ps. 119:130, The Message).

You may also desire to ask for help from a more mature believer.

Using your Bible or a commentary, briefly answer the following questions about Matthew 7:7.

To whom was this passage originally written?

_____

When? _____

Why? _____

How Am I to Experience the Passage Now?

Get specific. An ounce of application is worth a pound of abstraction. In the first two steps you study the Word. In application you let God's Word study you. Get uncomfortably specific in living what you've studied. God designed His Word to cause radical shifts in our direction as we apply it to our lives.

Ask yourself: *What does Matthew 7:7 say to me right now? What application can I make in my life?* **Write your answer on the following page.**

> The God who made, numbered, and named the stars ensured that the Scriptures never err in the truths they proclaim and explain.

_____

_____

I was paid very little to work part-time on a church staff. The pastor's charming father was retired, but he had been hired through his son to work with adults and to preach funerals. The older pastor routinely arrived at the office with bronzed skin from playing golf. I envied his recreation time and higher salary.

In my devotional time God surprised me with a verse:

As in water face reflects face,
So the heart of man reflects man (Prov. 27:19).

What does that say? I asked as I read it again. A face that is looking at still water is reflected back. God has wired us so that sometimes we can "just tell" that another person likes or hates us. People pick up our underlying attitudes and reflect them back to us. We get what we give!

Why was this verse written? In Old Testament times people didn't have mirrors as we do today, but the author, Solomon, had probably seen his reflection in pools of water or in ponds in the palace. The verse employs a figure of speech: your thoughts are mirrored to the hearts of others. What's inside is beaming out—like sonar from a submarine. No wonder God commands,

Watch over your heart with all diligence,
For from it flow the springs of life (Prov. 4:23).

At that point I wasn't sure how to experience the verse. The next day I stepped onto the church elevator. The older pastor was there, as tan as ever, and I recalled the verse. Uh-oh! Realizing that he would eventually detect my bitterness, I desperately punched an elevator floor button. "Why did you do that?" the pastor asked. "That's an empty floor." The doors opened, and I blurted out, "I'm meeting someone!" I did meet Someone. That floor was pitch dark like my heart! Dropping to my knees, I confessed to God my judgmental spirit.

God's Word is powerful.

God's Word is powerful. No wonder Paul calls the Bible "the sword of the Spirit" (Eph. 6:17). Ouch! The Holy Spirit will slice open your heart and will then give you spiritual surgery. Through that painful experience, however, the Father will give you great joy. Let God show you what to know, stop, change, or start.

Use the guidelines on the following page to interpret Scripture for your life.

10 Guidelines for Interpreting Scripture

1. *Live in harmony with the Author of the Book.* Be Spirit-filled, then Spirit-led (see John 7:17; 14:21 in the margin).
2. *Interpret Scripture with Scripture.* The Reformation began when Martin Luther came to a totally new insight about the Bible: no Scripture verse or passage can be interpreted so as to be in conflict with what is clearly taught elsewhere in the Bible.
3. *First interpret the Bible literally.* Accept the understood meaning. On the other hand, know the type of literature you are reading. Parables, prophecy, proverbs, poetry—all should be approached a bit differently. When Jesus said, " 'I am the true vine' " (John 15:1), He obviously didn't mean that He was literally a green vine! Our Lord illustrated different aspects of His character by using word-pictures.
4. *Erase the culture gap.* What is the historical background of the book or passage? Where did the author live? What approximate year was it?
5. *Keep in mind that a verse has one interpretation, one meaning, but multiple applications.* The verse's meaning has implications for today. For example, the commands in Ephesians 5:18, "Do not get drunk with wine, ... but be filled with the Spirit," imply a principle that we shouldn't be controlled by anything else, not just wine. Look for the simplest interpretation.
6. *Interpret a verse or a word by its context.*
7. *Define the meaning of a word by its first usage in a passage.* For example, the first use of *repentance* in Hebrews 6:1 means *repentance from dead works.* This defines the meaning of *repentance* when it is used later in verse 6.
8. *Read from multiple translations.* Give priority to the original languages; use any Greek or Hebrew helps you can. Make friends with a large concordance like *Strong's Exhaustive Concordance.* Or find the most complete concordance in a Bible computer program of your favorite translation. Book stores have tools that can help you dig deeper.
9. *Find the root meanings of key words.* For example, the meaning of *repentance* is *a change of attitude or mind.* Repenting produces a change of direction in us.
10. *Don't put God in a box.* Our earthly frame of reference is inadequate to fully understand the eternal. We "see in a mirror dimly" (1 Cor. 13:12). God has reserved secrets (see Deut. 29:29 in the margin). For example, can you imagine the streets of gold in heaven that are like glass (see Rev. 21:21)?

Jesus said, "If any man is willing to do His will, he shall know of the teaching, whether it is of God, or whether I speak from Myself" (John 7:17).

"He who has My commandments, and keeps them, he it is who loves Me; and he who loves Me shall be loved by My Father, and I will love him, and will disclose Myself to him" (John 14:21).

"The secret things belong to the Lord our God, but the things revealed belong to us and to our sons forever, that we may observe all the words of this law" (Deut. 29:29).

📖 Write Jeremiah 15:16 from memory in the margin. Then apply the passage, using the three questions you studied today: What does the passage say? Why was the passage written? How am I to experience the passage now? Make notes on a separate sheet of paper.

📖 Close in prayer. Thank God for giving you the ability and His Spirit to interpret His Word.

---

[1]Ben Campbell Johnson, *The Heart of Paul* (Waco, Tex.: Word, 1976), 8.

Day 5
You Are What You Eat

*W*hen you come to the banquet of the Bible, the Lord brings a sense of delight to your soul as you apply His Word. Say Jeremiah 15:16 aloud from memory before reading it below.

> *Thy words were found and I ate them,*
> *And Thy words became for me a joy and the delight of my heart;*
> *For I have been called by Thy name, O LORD God of hosts (Jer. 15:16).*

Like Jeremiah, David found satisfaction in God's Word:

> *I shall delight in Thy statutes;*
> *I shall not forget Thy Word (Ps. 119:16).*

Jesus Christ promises you joy when He answers your petitions: " 'Until now you have asked for nothing in My name; ask, and you will receive, that your joy may be made full' " (John 16:24).

When you have experiences with God in His Word, you gain other by-products besides the joy mentioned by Jeremiah, David, and Jesus. Answers to prayer, transformed attitudes, new insights, fresh growth, a sense of the Lord's presence—all flow from experiences with the written and the living Word. Be careful, though, about seeking feelings or miracles. Neither Bible facts nor fantastic emotions are your goal. Your goal should be to seek and know Christ!

Keep a Journal

It is rare to notice changes each day in your life. Still, whether or not you notice them regularly, the transition to be more like Christ occurs

When you come to the banquet of the Bible, the Lord brings a sense of delight to your soul as you apply His Word.

consistently. The tragedy is that few believers log the transforming adventures they undertake with the Father. My wife, Clemmie, has kept a prayer journal since we married. She records information in four columns: the date, the pressure situation, the prayer promise-verse, and the answer. I encourage you to keep a journal.

Practice writing a journal entry, using the outline suggested below.

Date: _____

Pressure situation: _____

_____

Prayer promise-verse: _____

_____

Answer: _____

_____

Claim God's Promises

"By these He has granted to us His precious and magnificent promises, in order that by them you might become partakers of the divine nature" (2 Pet. 1:4). Some scriptural promises are unconditional "blank checks" from God that faith can sign and cash. Other promises are conditional. You must do or be something in order for the Lord to fulfill the promise. For example,

> *"Come out from their midst and be separate, says the Lord.*
> . . . .
> *And I will welcome you.*
> *And I will be a father to you" (2 Cor. 6:17-18).*

Your obedient response is to "come out" from the world and be holy. Your promised reward is God's unique touch, fathering you and being close.

All of God's promises have a double meaning. First, they were for the persons He was addressing in Bible times. They can be promises for us too as the Holy Spirit guides us while we pray and wait before God. Remember, the Spirit links a specific promise to a need in your life, and He gives you the faith to believe that this promise is for you. But be careful to observe these guidelines:

Some scriptural promises are unconditional "blank checks" from God that faith can sign and cash.

These promises must be personalized by someone with a pure heart—the unselfish motive of wanting God to be glorified.

- God's promises are strictly in keeping with His character and nature.
- God's promises are in harmony with the rest of Scripture.
- These promises must be personalized by someone with a pure heart—the unselfish motive of wanting God to be glorified.

While I was in seminary, I pastored a small, country church in Cleburne, Texas. It was customary for friends of a dying person to relieve the family by sitting at night in the hospital room. One weekend I was asked to sit from midnight to 2:00 a.m. with a 30-year-old man who was related to a church member. He had been so tragically injured in a car accident that the funeral arrangements had already been made.

As I came in the room, the doctor was just leaving. He whispered, "He's not here long." I'd never seen anyone alive who looked that bad. At 1:00 a.m. I was doing my customary Bible reading when I came upon this passage: "Is anyone among you sick? Let him call for the elders of the church, and let them pray over him, anointing him with oil in the name of the Lord; and the prayer offered in faith will restore the one who is sick" (Jas. 5:14-15). I read it again, noting the Bible context. I closed my Bible. Feeling compelled, I opened it again, drawn to the promise. "Pray for his life," I heard God prompt me in my spirit.

I agreed to pray for healing from impending death. To follow the biblical instruction, I left the hospital at 1:45 a.m. in search of olive oil. Seeing a gas station open, I stopped and asked. The clerk laughed. "Olive oil? Yep, may be some in the back from an old store." He found a bottle!

Now I really was fearful. I'd never done this before, but I felt led to telephone our deacons to come and pray—now—for this dying man. Some agreed. In that hospital room I read the promise from James and put oil on the patient's forehead. The deacons and I earnestly prayed for God to heal him for the glory of God. I left to go to bed, and another person came to sit with him.

Later I was awakened by a phone call from a breathless relative. The young man had regained consciousness, sat up in bed, and requested coffee—right after I left the hospital. He eventually completely recovered.

By acting on God's scriptural promise to me, I found that God heals, using both prayer and medicine.

The Benefit of Eating

 Write Jeremiah 15:16 from memory in the margin.

The last line of Jeremiah 15:16 suggests that God's name and Jeremiah were associated. Eventually, Jeremiah became so identified with his God that people probably said, "There goes that Lord-God-of-hosts prophet." Scripture marks its home! Like a cattle rancher identifying his stock, God's Word had branded Jeremiah's life. And people couldn't miss seeing God in him.

In the first-century city of Antioch the general public coined a new term for followers of Christ: Christians (see Acts 11:26). Why did the citizens see these followers of Christ and identify them as such? Church starter and missionary Barnabas had "encouraged them all to remain true to the Lord with all their hearts" (Acts 11:23, NIV). Like Jeremiah, their actions and reputation were so linked with their Lord that nonbelievers referred to them by the name of their cause and their Leader.

The goal of our lives remains to be like Christ. This amazing merger—of Christ joined with you as you live His life—can't be hidden long. Your life lays the foundation for incredible witnessing opportunities! As you take up your cross daily (taking up God's will for your life; see 2 Cor. 4:10-11; 1 Pet. 4:1-2), others eventually make the connection and are confronted with the One who lives in you.

Do you dare to become identified with Jesus Christ? He speaks through a surrendered mouth. Jesus touches with hands that belong to Him. Jesus walks with feet entrusted to carry out His will. Jesus stimulates an aggressive love for others when your heart is His to minister. Jesus said that you bear fruit when you remain in Him and His words remain in you (see John 15:5-8). You can remain in Christ by feeding daily on His Word.

This week you have discovered the value of assimilating Scripture into your life. You have begun to develop tools for applying God's truths. The weeks that follow will build on this material as you learn how to apply God's Word in your daily life.

As you begin to truly "eat" the Word, generalization will give way to specific guidance. Truth and life will fuse in application. Bethlehem, Calvary, and the empty tomb will take on new meaning. And the Word will become flesh and blood again—in you!

What does God want you to do in response to this week's study? Choose an action or actions in the margin that you will commit to take. Write specific plans below.

_____

_____

Recite Jeremiah 15:16 as a closing thought for the week.

- ❏ **Begin or continue a daily quiet time.**
- ❏ **Spend more time each day studying the Word.**
- ❏ **Keep a journal.**
- ❏ **Study a Scripture passage in depth, using the guidelines on page 19.**
- ❏ **Study God's Word with more attention to life application.**
- ❏ **Memorize Scripture.**
- ❏ **Drink the milk of God's Word.**
- ❏ **Eat the meat of God's Word.**
- ❏ **Learn what God wants me to know.**
- ❏ **Stop doing something.**
- ❏ **Change something.**
- ❏ **Start doing something.**
- ❏ **Practice the three-step application process described in day 4 to examine a Scripture passage.**
- ❏ **Claim God's promises when I read Scripture.**
- ❏ **Apply and live God's truths.**

Week 2
The Surprising Habit That Changes Your Life

Day 1
The Miracle Verse

FOCUS
This week you will consider why Scripture memorization is important for Christian growth and will practice a proven process of Scripture memorization.

MEMORY VERSES
I can do all things through Him who strengthens me (Phil. 4:13).

"Until now you have asked for nothing in My name; ask, and you will receive, that your joy may be made full" (John 16:24).

*T*here is a powerful habit so simple that a child can do it. It seems so elementary, however, that most adults *aren't* doing it. Satan has masked its life-changing potential. This practice is the fastest way to link Scripture to your life to bring about change. Besides your daily quiet time with God, this habit is the best way to propel you into a dynamic pattern of spiritual growth. Let me introduce this habit with a story.

Years ago I was in a packed retreat listening to Dawson Trotman, a Billy Graham Evangelism Team member, relate this intriguing personal experience. It was 1948. Civil war had broken out in China. In less than two years China would be controlled by the Communists, and millions would die. Miss Jones, a missionary to China, had completed her furlough in the United States and was ready to return to the mission field. After accompanying Miss Jones to the ship, Trotman prayed with her in her cabin before she departed.

Within two years Miss Jones was in prison under great pressure. Chinese businessmen, pastors, and missionaries were being killed daily. Christians all over the world prayed for the release of missionaries still in China. Finally, all foreigners were banished. Miss Jones was on one of the first planes out.

"Miss Jones from China is here!" Trotman's secretary shouted as she opened his office door. "She just got off the plane." Trotman rushed out to greet his frail-looking friend. He brought her into his office and listened as they drank tea together.

"I just had to stop by on the way home—to thank you," Miss Jones said.

"No need to thank me," said Trotman. "I prayed for you as many others did."

Miss Jones, with deep emotion, whispered, "What you said four years ago on board ship before I left for China saved my life."

"What did I say?" asked Trotman.

Miss Jones related her horrific ordeal. "I was tortured by the Communists, who encouraged us to kill ourselves. Many gave in. I thought of it, but every time I nearly gave up, what you'd said popped into my mind. Just after you prayed in my cabin, you shared a verse of Scripture for me to take to China. I memorized it while traveling across the Pacific. God used it powerfully, shielding me from suicide. Thank you. That verse saved my life."

When our speaker's message was over, many of us ran to the front of the auditorium. "Give us that verse," we urged. Trotman questioned, "Why do you want the verse?" We said, "What a counseling verse for someone who is depressed!" He paused. Finally, he announced: "I'm not going to give you the verse." "Why?" I yelled over the crowd. "Because there are hundreds of them!"

Trotman was right, of course. God's Word contains thousands of verses that can work like a miracle drug to bring new life to a hurting person. His silence caused us to reconsider the power of a single verse to change our lives if we adopted a lifelong habit. The habit that will change your life is Scripture memorization, coupled with meditation. Trotman knew that any verse can be a miracle verse when someone: (1) has the heart to memorize and live it and (2) follows God's prompting to pass it on.

Nothing I've done in 40 years of ministry has consistently been so productive, so broad in its payoff for the time spent, as the habit of memorizing verses. This week I want to share five reasons I find Scripture memorization valuable in my life. I also want to teach you my method of memorization. Next week we will couple memorization with meditation.

Reason 1: Handling Pressure

Most of us will never encounter the pressure Miss Jones experienced inside a jail cell in China. However, in your lifetime you'll encounter change, the unexpected, and stresses affecting yourself and those you love. At these junctures Scripture in your heart is like an emergency-room doctor who applies the right procedures to a bloodied patient at a critical time.

Dawson Trotman challenged that crowded room, "What if I hadn't had the arrow of God's Word in the quiver of my heart so that the Holy Spirit could fit it to the bow of my lips and send it to a ready heart?" Someone you know is going through a crisis. Nothing is as beneficial as sharing with a wounded person a special word from the Wonderful Counselor. Read Proverbs 15:23 in the margin.

In 1993 a massive brain hemorrhage killed our son Paul. We helplessly watched as death snatched the last minutes of his 28 years on earth. The Holy Spirit used memorized verses to remind us of our Father's love:

A man has joy in an apt answer,
And how delightful is a timely
word! (Prov. 15:23).

"I have loved you with an everlasting love;
Therefore I have drawn you with lovingkindness" (Jer. 31:3).

"In all their distress he too was distressed,
and the angel of his presence saved them.
In his love and mercy he redeemed them;
he lifted them up and carried them" (Isa. 63:9, NIV).

" 'I will never desert you, nor will I ever forsake you' " (Heb. 13:5).

Our tears were mixed with hope and peace. Because our son was a believer, we'll see him again at the resurrection. Memorized Scripture helped us through those days.

Steps to Successful Scripture Memorization
Today and tomorrow I will share with you my method of Scripture memorization. First, let's perform an attitude check.

What is your attitude about memorizing Scripture? Check all that apply.
❏ I tried and quit.   ❏ I often memorize Scripture.
❏ I don't see the value in it.   ❏ I don't have time.
❏ I can't do it.   ❏ I want to learn to do it.

If your responses were less than positive, you are ready for step 1:

Step 1: Begin with a positive attitude.

Start with a positive attitude. People mistakenly rationalize, "I just can't memorize." My response is "Then cut Philippians 4:13 out of your Bible. It doesn't work." Although the apostle Paul affirmed, "I can do all things through Him who strengthens me," the devil has tricked people into thinking that they can't memorize Scripture. We constantly memorize—telephone numbers, keys on our key ring, or names of lipstick shades. You can learn to memorize verses for a lifetime. If you memorize just two verses a week, in a year you'll learn more than one hundred. In 10 years you'll know more than one thousand verses!

❏ I make a commitment to memorize two verses this week. ❏ I can't make this commitment now but will remain open to God's leadership as I continue this week's study.

If you made that commitment, I will lead you to memorize Philippians 4:13 and John 16:24, which are printed in the margin from the *New American Standard Bible*. Read them today from the margin or from

I can do all things through Him who strengthens me (Phil. 4:13).

"Until now you have asked for nothing in My name; ask, and you will receive, that your joy may be made full" (John 16:24).

another translation if you prefer. Tomorrow I will share with you the remaining steps that have worked for me.

🌿 **Close today's study with a prayer in which you commit to God your decision to memorize Scripture.**

Day 2
Lighting a Dark Path

*H*ave you ever hiked in the woods on a moonless night? Twigs crack beneath your shoes. Could it be a snake? Leaves rustle in the bushes. What's out there? It's so dark, and the path is unclear. You're grateful for even a tiny flashlight.

Reason 2: Getting Guidance

A second reason for making Scripture memorization a habit is to get guidance and direction for your life. The psalmist compared the Bible to a light on a dark trail. Read his words in the margin.

The foggy and detour-riddled roads of life can be just as difficult to trek as a trail on a dark night. However, if you memorize and apply one verse, it's like having a penlight to guide you. If you know 10 verses of Scripture, you have a flashlight beam on the road. With 100 verses you've got headlights. Know 1,000 verses of Scripture and wow! You go through life with a football stadium bank of lights surrounding your every move, bringing God's clarity and definition to circumstances. Verses I've learned have brought dazzling light to decisions and behavior patterns that were previously in the dark: "Your ears will hear a word behind you, 'This is the way, walk in it,' whenever you turn to the right or to the left" (Isa. 30:21).

🌿 **What are the two reasons I've given so far for making Scripture memorization a habit for spiritual growth?**

Reason 1: _____

Reason 2: _____

Passing the Test

When I was a seminary student, my evangelism professor required us to memorize 300 verses of Scripture. From the start of the semester he warned us about our final exam: "If you fail the Scripture-memorization section of the exam, you will flunk the whole course."

By your words I can see where I'm going;
they throw a beam of light on my dark path.
I've committed myself and I'll never turn back (Ps. 119:105, The Message).

The unfolding of Thy words gives light;
It gives understanding to the simple (Ps. 119:130).

I rationalized, *It's stupid to try to learn 300 verses in three months.* I carefully picked and learned 25 verses. I picked the wrong ones! I failed the course in evangelism because my heart wasn't into the habit of memorizing Scripture.

The following summer I had an experience that changed my attitude about memorizing Scripture. I'll share that later in the week. First, let me share the remaining steps to successfully recall any verse anytime.

Try to maintain quality by mastering each verse.

The goal of a Scripture-memorization program is not to memorize as many verses as possible. Try to maintain quality by mastering each verse rather than sacrificing quality for quantity. The following steps should facilitate a balance.

Step 2: Glue the reference to the first words.

Have you noticed how frequently Christians say, "The verse goes like this, … but I can't remember where it's found"? You can avoid this common problem by "gluing" the reference to the first words of the verse. Say the reference and the first words without pausing. For example, "John 16:24—Until now you have asked." That way you'll always be able to find any memorized Bible verse.

Repeat three times the references and first phrases in Philippians 4:13.

Step 3: Memorize bite by bite.

Next, repeat the verse to the first punctuation mark, ending with the reference. For example, "John 16:24—Until now you have asked for nothing in My name—John 16:24." Say that over and over. Then repeat what you have learned and add the next phrase, still starting and ending with the reference. Memorize a verse the way you eat a 10-ounce steak—bite by bite, phrase by phrase. It's easier because you are learning only five or six words at a time. Learn the verse word-perfect in any translation you want. If your verse has a topic, follow this order: topic, reference, verse, reference.

Learn Philippians 4:13 phrase by phrase. Repeat the verse aloud. Use the verse printed on page 24 from the *New American Standard Bible* or a translation of your choice.

Step 4: Review, review, review.

The master secret to memorization is review, review, review. Write each verse on a small card to use in review. Blank business cards or language-review cards are available at book stores. Say the verses as quickly and accurately as possible; meditation is a separate step. After memorizing, review the verse every day for 90 days. The best review is using the verse in your life or to help another person. Use it or lose it!

Write **Philippians 4:13** on a note card. Carry it with you this week and review it often.

Step 5: Meditate on the verse(s).

Meditate on each verse the week you learn it. Ultimately, you want to experience Christ as that verse's truth works in you. Keep thinking how this verse can be lived. I memorize a new verse on Mondays and Wednesdays. On Tuesdays and Thursdays I meditate on the verses memorized. Daily I review new and old verses. Linking the two disciplines of memorization and meditation gives the Holy Spirit an amazing scalpel to remake heart, life, and attitudes. You will learn how to meditate next week.

Experience Christ as the verse's truth works in you.

Step 6: Use spare time wisely.

Utilize your spare time to learn and review. Carry a pack of memory cards with you while you exercise or wait in line. My wife learned her first hundred verses at an ironing board. Clemmie also puts verse cards on the window sill behind the kitchen sink. Sometimes I put a current verse on the dash of the car to review while stopped at traffic lights.

List the best places and times in your daily schedule for learning and reviewing Scripture.

_____

_____

Step 7: Team with a friend.

Team with someone else who is memorizing Scripture. Listen to each other's verse, following along in the Bible to check accuracy.

Step 8: Use a Scripture-memorization system.

Finally, select a tested system as a guideline. The Navigators' *Topical Memory System* is a proven tool for memorizing successfully. During a critical time in my life, God changed me as I used this verses-a-week system, organized by topics. Other good programs are available for children, youth, and adults.[1]

Let's review the eight steps for successful Scripture memorization. Fill in the missing words.

1. Begin with a _____ attitude.

2. Glue the _____ to the _____ words.

3. Memorize _____ by _____.

4. _____, _____, _____.

5. _____ on the verse(s).

6. Use _____ _____ wisely.

7. Team with a _____.

8. Use a _____-_____ system.

If necessary, go back and check your answers in today's and yesterday's material.

The time will come when you will undergo a crucial test on Scripture memorization. It may not be an exam taken at seminary or Bible school. The test will come when God's Spirit offers you an opportunity to meet a need in someone's life through a verse. Because you are writing God's Word on your heart through Scripture memorization, I believe that you'll pass this crucial test with flying colors.

The test will come when God's Spirit offers you an opportunity to meet a need in someone's life through a verse.

---

[1]In the *Building Disciples* notebook I have provided 36 verses for memory. Order from Missions Unlimited; P.O. Box 8203; Tampa, FL 33674-8203. Many of these parallel verses can be found in the Navigators' *Topical Memory System* (Colorado Springs, Colo.: NavPress, 1981).

Day 3
Winning over Temptation

God does not want us to repeat the same sin over and over. Psalm 119:11 affirms:

Thy word I have treasured in my heart,
That I may not sin against Thee.

The Holy Spirit will bring to mind a well-treasured verse in a time of temptation to help us stand firm.

The law of his God is in his heart;
His steps do not slip (Ps. 37:31).

Memorizing Scripture helps us not to slip.

Reason 3: Gaining Victory over Sin

Because I speak often in my ministry, it is easier for me to sin with my speech. I must guard against being inaccurate, overwhelming, or out of balance. I once asked a man who holds his tongue well, "What is your secret?" He said that he read through the Books of Proverbs and James, looking for every verse about speech and the tongue. Then, he prayerfully chose verses to memorize during a three-month period: Proverbs 12:18; 15:1,28; 17:27-28; 18:21; 21:23; 22:11; 25:15; and James 3. His verses have also had an impact on me.

Jesus' Model

Jesus modeled for us His amazing plan for withstanding Satan's attack. Jesus was in the wilderness praying and fasting (see Matt. 4; Luke 4). Without warning, Satan appeared to tempt Him.

How vulnerable are you at your weakest moment? Briefly describe an experience in which you were vulnerable to temptation.

_____

_____

Jesus was just as vulnerable—to self-interest and to sin. He'd been without food for 40 days and nights. His stomach was empty, and His energy was low.

The tempter was obviously aware of Jesus' need. He said, " 'If You are the Son of God, command that these stones become bread' " (Matt. 4:3). In Greek *if* in this passage actually means *since.* The devil knew that Jesus had the power of God's Son. To this first trap, a hungry Jesus responded, " 'It is written, "Man shall not live on bread alone, but on every word that proceeds out of the mouth of God" ' " (Matt. 4:4).

Twice more the tempter approached Jesus with attractive offers to the human heart: pride and instant power. For his second attack, Satan copied Jesus and tried to outwit Him by quoting verses, too. But Satan misquoted verses and took verses out of context. He told Jesus to throw Himself from the huge temple in Jerusalem, quoting Psalm 91:11-12.

Jesus modeled for us His amazing plan for withstanding Satan's attack.

Jesus replied: " 'On the other hand, it is written, "You shall not put the Lord your God to the test" ' " (Matt. 4:7).

Taking Jesus to a high mountain and showing Him the kingdoms of the world, Satan continued: " 'All these things will I give You, if You fall down and worship me.' " Jesus responded, " 'Begone, Satan! For it is written, "You shall worship the Lord your God, and serve Him only" ' " (Matt. 4:10).

All three times Jesus countered Satan with God's Word, quoting from the Book of Deuteronomy (see Deut. 8:3; 6:16,13). Why did Jesus quote Scripture when every word He spoke was the Word of God? Think of it! He could have simply said, "Get lost!" That would have been the authoritative Word of God. Instead, Jesus quoted God's Word as a model for us. Undoubtedly, Jesus later told His disciples about the devil's attack and His scriptural response. Jesus told them to teach the value of having God's Word in their hearts. He didn't have victory just by quoting verses. His heart was surrendered to God's principles contained in each verse, which shielded Him against the temptation.

What is the devil's strategy? To keep you from experiencing Scripture as "living and active and sharper than any two-edged sword, and piercing as far as the division of soul and spirit ... to judge the thoughts and intentions of the heart" (Heb. 4:12). With God's Word treasured inside, you can walk away from the enemy's seductive offers.

Write from memory in the margin Philippians 4:13. Then, on a separate sheet of paper, answer the following questions about the verse: What does it say? Why was it written? How am I to experience it now? What is this verse calling me to know, stop, change, or do?

Memorize John 16:24, using the steps you have learned. Use the verse printed on page 24 from the *New American Standard Bible* or a translation of your choice.

To Be like Jesus

My primary motivation for memorizing Scripture is to get to know Christ and to follow my Lord. Who wouldn't want to be like our fearless, powerful, yet gentle Lord Jesus? Maybe we can't walk on water, but we can imitate the Lord in His powerful habit of memorizing Scripture. In Matthew's Gospel alone Christ is recorded to have quoted Old Testament verses 89 times (35 direct citations, 54 allusions).[1] Jesus, the living Word, placed within His heart the written Word.

Read Colossians 3:16 in the margin. "Richly dwell"—you must be saturated with Christ's thoughts and words for that rich indwelling to take place. His Word is not to be like a house guest but rather like a family member who moves in permanently. Scripture memorization

Let the word of Christ richly dwell within you, with all wisdom teaching and admonishing one another (Col. 3:16).

allows you to flood your mind with Jesus' mind—His strength under criticism, His world vision, His love for enemies, His compassion for the lost and brokenhearted. The Holy Spirit says, "Have this attitude [mind] in yourselves which was also in Christ Jesus" (Phil. 2:5). You can flood your mind with His by hiding His Word in your heart.

Close today's study with a prayer in which you thank God for the power of His Word to overcome temptation.

---

[1]Graham Scroggie, *A Guide to the Gospels* (Westwood, N.J.: Fleming H. Revell Co., 1948), 270.

Day 4
Witnessing and Discipleship Made Simple

*M*y future wife was finishing a subspecialty at Baylor Medical in Houston. In the 15 years since being saved, Clemmie had never been an effective verbal witness. Then she attended a retreat where we first met. I was the speaker and taught how to witness. After that weekend Clemmie memorized witnessing verses in a simple witnessing illustration. Prayerfully, she began giving her salvation testimony to friends at the hospital.

With each friend who showed interest, Clemmie drew the illustration on a paper napkin in the cafeteria. Carefully, she quoted with meaning each gospel verse. At each encounter she asked her friend to receive Christ. Within a couple of weeks she had presented the gospel to six persons. Two of her friends invited Christ into their hearts. The only thing new in her life was those few memorized verses, waiting for an opportunity. You can guess the rest of the story. I was so impressed. It went beyond her beauty and gracious Southern sparkle. Clemmie was eager to learn God's Word, and she had a teachable, hungry heart for Christ. So I talked her into marrying me!

Reason 4: Making Witnessing and Discipleship Simple

Scripture memorization makes witnessing simple and replaces fear with quiet boldness. The gospel story is revealed in Scripture. Memorizing key verses in a gospel presentation unleashes a timid tongue to share the good news. You may not have the opportunity to open a Bible, but memorized Scriptures give you flexibility to witness to anyone anywhere anytime.

I've seen church members who had never been successful in evangelism begin to boldly share the gospel after memorizing key verses. All

Memorized Scriptures give you flexibility to witness to anyone anywhere anytime.

of those who persisted bore fruit. The more people in my church who memorized the good news, the more fruitful witnessing we experienced as a fellowship. "Now as they observed the confidence of Peter and John, and understood that they were uneducated and untrained men, they were marveling, and began to recognize them as having been with Jesus" (Acts 4:13).

Jesus' Disciples Picked Up the Habit

Jesus' closest followers memorized Scripture. A copy of the Law and the Prophets (our Old Testament) was guardedly placed in the synagogues that could afford one. The Old Testament had no pocket editions—only heart editions. For three years the disciples listened to Jesus quote, illustrate, and demonstrate the Old Testament. His followers rediscovered Moses and the Prophets with fresh intimacy. They were made mighty by both the words and life of Christ.

Because Jesus used memorized Scriptures to disciple His followers, it is not surprising that Matthew used 129 references from the Old Testament.[1] Mark, who was mentored by the apostle Peter, used 63 references in his book.[2] The Acts, written by Luke, uses over 200 Old Testament quotations.[3]

 Write John 16:24 from memory in the margin.

Family Impact

Witnessing and discipleship begin at home. Scripture memorization, coupled with meditation, can almost disaster-proof your kids. Begin when they are young. If Mom and Dad set the pace, the children will enjoy memorization. Families can discuss one memory verse a week and can have fun imagining how to put it to use. Also, the bond between husband and wife grows stronger as they memorize, share insights, and pray together. Times like this will greatly shorten the gap between head knowledge and life learning.

The marketplace, university, or military can chew up a godly child if he or she is unprepared to face temptations. Before leaving home, your child should master at least 50 to 100 verses. God will use these to show your child the consequences of breaking God's Word and ways to escape sin. Without this tool of the Holy Spirit, what chance do our children have against the world system, the flesh, and the devil?

 Does your family have a plan for Scripture memorization? Try using the following outline to plan for Scripture memorization in your home.

Time: _____

> **Scripture memorization, coupled with meditation, can almost disaster-proof your kids.**

Place: _____

Process: _____

_____

Goal: To memorize _____ verses per _____

Consider the Context

As your memorization skills grow, you may want to memorize longer passages. The fastest way to remember lengthy sections of the Bible is to memorize a key verse in each chapter or section. Peg down the context with a verse. If you carefully link that verse in your mind to its context, you can easily recall the subject of the whole chapter. For instance, many people have memorized John 3:16. The context is a witnessing conversation Jesus had with Nicodemus. In this classic passage Jesus explained the major concept of being born again.

🌿 **If you want to go the extra mile, fill your heart with verses from John's Gospel that reveal the character and titles of Christ or that highlight the main emphases of the chapters. Begin this now or after completing *Living God's Word*. Memorize at least one verse in each chapter.**

- John 1:12-14—Word
- John 2:5—authority
- John 3:3,16-17—new birth
- John 4:34-35—white harvest
- John 5:24,39—life
- John 6:29,35—Bread of life
- John 7:37-38—living water
- John 8:12—Light
- John 8:31-32—disciples
- John 9:4,31—work
- John 10:4,9—Door
- John 11:25-26—resurrection
- John 12:24-26,32—followers
- John 13:13-14,17—servants
- John 14:2-3,6—Way
- John 15:5,7-8—Vine
- John 16:8-11—Holy Spirit
- John 17:3—eternal life
- John 18:11—cup
- John 19:17-18—cross
- John 20:21,31—Son of God
- John 21:16—love and shepherd

I recommend memorizing individual verses initially. It is more practical to have memorized, at the end of one year, 52 verses from topics throughout the Bible than two entire chapters. Through the balance that a breadth of Scripture provides, you'll have sure footing on life's road.

🌿 **What are the four reasons I've given for making Scripture memorization a habit for spiritual growth?**

Reason 1: _____

> **Through the balance that a breadth of Scripture provides, you'll have sure footing on life's road.**

Reason 2: _____

Reason 3: _____

Reason 4: _____

🌿 Close today's study with a prayer in which you ask God to make you sensitive to opportunities to share Scriptures with others as you share your faith.

---

[1]Graham Scroggie, *A Guide to the Gospels* (Westwood, N.J.: Fleming H. Revell Co., 1948), 270.
[2]Ibid., 190.
[3]Montgomery, *The Twentieth Century New Testament*, rev. ed. (New York: Fleming H. Revell Co., 1904).

Day 5
Answering Prayers

*M*any people don't get answers to prayer because they are ignorant of God's principles. The Lord has established certain guidelines for answered prayer:
- Ask with sins confessed (see Ps. 66:18; Prov. 28:9).
- Ask by faith (see Matt. 21:22).
- Ask in Jesus' name (see John 16:24).
- Ask according to His will (see 1 John 5:14-15).

Reason 5: Receiving Answers to Prayers

"If you abide in Me, and My words abide in you, ask whatever you wish, and it shall be done for you" (John 15:7).

A final reason to memorize God's Word is to get answers to prayer. Read Jesus' words in the margin and notice the conditions for getting answers to prayer: (1) abiding in Christ and (2) His Word's abiding, staying, living in you! Prayer power is always linked to God's will and Word.

The summer after I flunked my evangelism class, I hitchhiked from Fort Worth, Texas, to Chicago, Illinois. There I worked with Pacific Garden Mission, a terrific organization ministering to alcoholics and servicemen on skid row. Dennis Snell was a giant of God there who greatly influenced my life. This former navy man lived the Bible more than anyone I'd been around. One day I asked Dennis, "How do you know so much Bible and have a great attitude about work?" He said, "Well, I guess it's from spending two hours a day in the Bible for four years and hiding God's Word in my heart."

"What?" I was shocked. "You spend two hours a day in the Bible and you're not a preacher?" Dennis laughed. "Hiding God's Word in your heart?" I asked. "You mean … memorizing Scripture?" "Yes." "I hate to memorize Scripture," I confessed. "It's a waste of time." He replied: "I'm not going to argue with you. I'm just telling you that it changed my life."

I watched Dennis for two or three more days. Then I went to him. "You have something I need. Teach me how to memorize Scripture." "You don't really want to memorize!" he said. I convinced him that I was serious. "All right," Dennis responded, "go talk to God. If you believe that God wants you to memorize, then make a commitment to Him and tell me. If the Lord is leading you, then He will keep you at it when I'm not around." Feeling convicted, I surrendered in prayer to make this a growth habit in my life.

The next day I reported to Dennis, who smiled and said, "I'm going to give you four great verses to meet Satan's first four attacks on a new Christian." *Hey, this is practical,* I thought. As I memorized, Dennis asked me searching questions about the verses' content, meanings, and possible application. He wanted me to digest those verses.

Read in your Bible the following verses, which confront Satan's first attacks on a Christian. Recite John 16:24, which you memorized this week.
- **Assurance of salvation—1 John 5:11-12**
- **Assurance of answered prayer—John 16:24**
- **Assurance of victory—1 Corinthians 10:13**
- **Assurance of forgiveness—1 John 1:9**

Because I had hitchhiked to Chicago, my shoes were worn out. I woke up one morning and realized that I had holes in the bottoms of my shoes. I had no money. The mission gave me only room and board. My family couldn't support me: my father was dead, and my mother had entered an institution after his sudden death. Christ was lovingly drawing me to Himself; His promises were to be my supply.

First, I tried a piece of cardboard inside my shoes. But it rained, and the cardboard disintegrated. That morning I was learning and meditating on John 16:24: " 'Until now you have asked for nothing in My name; ask, and you will receive, that your joy may be made full.' " Ask and receive. Was a big God interested in the holes in my shoes? As I reread the verse, I felt that God wanted me to ask Him for a solution to my beat-up shoes.

I checked at Sears and found that I could get a pair of thin foam-rubber shoe soles for 15 cents. I didn't even have 15 cents. I began to pray. It took me three days of memorizing and quoting the verse to actually believe that God would somehow provide the 15 cents.

One morning I was handing out gospel tracts on the street in front of our building. My buddy Ray Miner walked up. Ray flipped a coin in my direction as he walked into our facilities, saying: "Catch this! Go get a milk shake." It was a quarter! I was ecstatic: "Here is God's answer to prayer—15 cents for the shoe soles and a dime tip!"

Christ was lovingly drawing me to Himself; His promises were to be my supply.

At lunch I told the fellows about it. One guy at the table was a converted alcoholic who worked at the mission. He asked my shoe size. I said: "I wear a 12. Why?" "I was just curious." That afternoon I was back outside handing out tracts. About 3:30 that same man shoved a package into my back pocket. I heard the cellophane crinkle. "What are you doing?" I questioned. "I want an investment in your big feet. Here are your shoe soles."

This was getting good. Now I had the shoe soles and a quarter. "Thank You, Lord!" That night I pulled out the instructions. I put on a layer of glue. Then I patted down the thin soles over my shoes' holes. I found some shoe polish and quickly shined my wonderful worn-out shoes.

The next morning I walked downstairs in my praying shoes. I was walking on John 16:24! I quoted the verse in rhythm with my steps: "Ask, and you will receive, … that your joy … may be made full, … that your joy … may be made full." I had a duet with a promise from God! I walked to the mission library and began reading my Bible.

The associate director came by. "Hey, Waylon," he said, "those shoes you have on look awful!" I was puzzled. I hadn't realized that the only thing holding the shoes together were the shoelaces and new shoe soles. He told me to get $10.00 from the mission office and buy a new pair of shoes at a bargain shop. I paid $7.98 for the shoes and gave a $2.02 offering to the Lord.

I asked the Lord for shoe soles, and He gave me shoes! "Now to Him who is able to do exceeding abundantly beyond all that we ask or think" (Eph. 3:20).

From that experience on, I began to see that the Bible was for "eating," not just "smelling." The habit of Scripture memorization propelled me from being a potential dead-in-the-water-Christian into exciting adventures with God. Coupled with meditation, it is the catalyst to the Word's becoming flesh in us.

What does God want you to do in response to this week's study? Check all of the responses in the margin that apply.

Close this week's study by reciting from memory Philippians 4:13 and John 16:24.

❑ Develop a positive attitude toward Scripture memorization.

❑ Make a commitment to memorize God's Word.

❑ Practice a Scripture-memorization process that is effective for me.

❑ Memorize _____ verses of Scripture each _____.

❑ Memorize verses from John's Gospel that reveal the character and titles of Christ.

❑ Memorize the four verses that equip us to confront Satan's attacks.

Week 3
An Unexpected Source of Success

Day 1
Seeing a Verse from the Outside In

*O*nce I had the opportunity to lead the music for revival services at the church my cousin pastored in Pearland, Texas. Something happened that week that changed my life.

For our first visit during the revival, we went to pray with the Johnsons. The husband was the deacon chairman at the church my cousin pastored. A few months earlier the Johnsons' daughter had died in childbirth, leaving a healthy new baby, a toddler, a devastated husband, and her parents. Mrs. Johnson was very ill, out of touch with reality.

As we drove, my cousin told me that the Johnsons were on edge, waiting for a bed in a mental hospital for Mrs. Johnson. He warned me, "Just act natural—no matter what Mrs. Johnson does." I got scared.

When we were inside the house, Mrs. Johnson walked into the room toward me. Dressed in a housecoat, she looked dazed and heavily medicated. She grabbed me by the shoulder. Her voice was monotone and pathetic: "Look—at—my—daughter. Isn't—she—beautiful?" She showed me a photo of her daughter's body in a casket. A picture of a casket? I tried to pull away. "Look—at—my—daughter." She stared me in the eyes until I felt forced to take the photo. "Uh, that's a nice colored photo," I stumbled to find words. Mrs. Johnson kept holding on to me as my cousin began to pray for her. Afterward, Mr. Johnson lovingly held her, and we quietly excused ourselves and left.

To get the impact of what happened next, you need to know where I was in my journey with God at that point in my life. I had been concentrating on making my time with God more practical. I had asked ministers what it means to meditate on Scripture, and I had read biographies of men of God who did this. Through study I began to formulate steps to meditate on Scripture.

🌿 **How would you define *meditation*?** _____

_____

Followers of Eastern religions and New Age cults practice a mindless form of meditation in an effort to discover what they believe to be a

THIS WEEK'S LESSONS
Day 1: Seeing a Verse from the Outside In
Day 2: Beyond Bible Reading
Day 3: The Process of Pulverizing
Day 4: Glue the Promise to the Problem
Day 5: Put Yourself in the Verse

FOCUS
This week you will understand how meditation facilitates Christian growth and will develop the practice of meditation in your spiritual life.

MEMORY VERSES
Casting all your anxiety upon Him, because He cares for you (1 Pet. 5:7).

His delight is in the law of the Lord,
And in His law he meditates day and night.
And he will be like a tree firmly planted by streams of water,
Which yields its fruit in its season,
And its leaf does not wither;
And in whatever he does, he prospers (Ps. 1:2-3).

divinity that lies hidden within themselves. Christian meditation, however, is neither mindless nor self-centered. Meditation is reflective thinking with a view to application. You think about God's ways and align your heart with His will and purpose. The Greek word for *meditate* means *to attend*.[1] It requires reading with attention to what the Scripture really says. Meditation opens Scripture the way a knife splits a watermelon. I have learned that meditation can be done in five steps, each including a word that begins with the letter *p*.

> Step 1: Understand the *perimeter* of the verse.
> Step 2: *Paraphrase* the verse.
> Step 3: *Pulverize* the verse.
> Step 4: *Personalize* the verse.
> Step 5: *Pray* the verse into your life.

Step 1: Understand the Perimeter of the Verse

The meaning of a verse is colored and revealed by the verses that surround it.

Look at the perimeter of the verse as you meditate. The meaning of a verse is colored and revealed by the verses that surround it. We can compare this step to a hamburger. The "meat" is the verse you choose for meditation. Surrounding the meat patty is the context—sauce, lettuce, cheese, pickles, and onions on a bun! You can eat a burger without the fixings, but who wants to? In the same way, you can study a verse without taking into account its context. But if you miss the meaning of the perimeter, you will lose the verse's flavor and perspective.

That night in Pearland I was meditating on 1 Peter 5:7, which I had memorized. I was examining it in light of its context—understanding the perimeter.

Open your Bible to 1 Peter 5:7, a simple verse for learning how to meditate. Repeat it three times. Now read verses 1-14 to get the flavor of the verse. On a separate sheet of paper write a summary of the truths you find in verses 1-14. What new perspective do you get about the meaning of verse 7 from its context?

When I read 1 Peter 5:7 for the first time with its perimeter, I was astonished by the link between verses 7 and 8: "Casting all your anxiety upon Him, because He cares for you. Be of sober spirit, be on the alert. Your adversary, the devil, prowls about like a roaring lion, seeking someone to devour." Why were these two verses placed together? God showed me a cause-effect relationship between casting burdens on the Lord and escaping the lion, Satan: cast all your anxiety or get eaten alive!

Just then my thoughts turned to Mrs. Johnson. The weight of losing her daughter had overwhelmed her. That photo symbolized a burden she couldn't or wouldn't cast away. What would happen if she, by faith, gave her daughter to God, surrendering the right to have her on earth?

Have you experienced 1 Peter 5:7? Do you need to apply it to your life right now? Identify an anxiety (a person, problem, or pressure) that you are experiencing. Throughout the week I will guide you through a process of turning that anxiety over to God. Describe your anxiety.

I'd never dealt with a situation like this before but was captivated by this Scripture. I had to call my cousin. He arranged for an appointment with the family the next morning. We arrived at the house, a sleepy music director and a pastor. I'd stayed up half the night praying. As we came into the room, Mrs. Johnson again showed me the photo and grabbed my arm. "Let's sit down, Mrs. Johnson," I suggested. I communicated my sympathy. Then I acted on what I'd learned from meditating: "Mrs. Johnson, your daughter trusted in Christ. She was never in that casket. The Bible says, 'To be absent from the body … [is] to be at home with the Lord' (2 Cor. 5:8). She's with Jesus, but you're trying to keep her here. Let's pray, and you give your precious girl to the Lord."

Mrs. Johnson moaned and began to cry. I led her in a prayer thanking the Lord that her daughter was with Him in heaven and releasing her to His care. Mr. Johnson prayed, too, and then the pastor. Then Mrs. Johnson stood up and looked around. She spoke with more focus as she declared, "I feel different." Her eyes seemed clear. The pastor said, "I believe that God has brought health to our sister." I was dazed. Had God healed this woman? I regularly checked on Mrs. Johnson over the next year. She recovered and was caring for her grandchildren. She had fully cast her care on the Lord!

If you understand the perimeter as you meditate on Scripture, verses will jump off the pages of your Bible into the clay of your life.

Begin memorizing your Scripture for the week. Using the process you learned last week, memorize 1 Peter 5:7 today. Use the verse printed on page 39 from the *New American Bible* or choose another translation.

Close today's study by reading Psalm 1:2-3 in your Bible or on page 39. Pray, asking God to guide you this week as you learn to meditate on His Word.

> If you understand the perimeter as you meditate on Scripture, verses will jump off the pages of your Bible into the clay of your life.

[1]W. H. Griffith Thomas, as quoted by Wilbur M. Smith, *Profitable Bible Study,* 2nd rev. ed. (Natick, Mass.: W. A. Wilde Co., 1963), 62.

Day 2
Beyond Bible Reading

*M*editation is reflective thinking with a view to living God's will as revealed in Scripture. God Himself invented the discipline of meditation. Unfortunately, Eastern religions have cleverly exported their brand of it, so that many Christians shy away from meditating on the Word. Biblical meditation is not clearing the mind of thought, as some religions teach. Our Teacher is the Holy Spirit. In meditation God's Spirit leads us to focus our minds on the living Lord revealed in the Word.

Meditation is as different from Bible reading as a one-way side street is from an eight-lane freeway. Reading is a one-way street, whereas meditation involves "two-way traffic."[1] You encounter the living God, hearing His voice and learning from Him. At the same time, you respond to Him in prayer. Meditation's goal is a oneness with the living Lord.

God considers meditation so important that He commands us to do it. In the original Hebrew, one word for *meditate* in Scripture is *hagah*. The word is first found in Joshua 1:8, which appears in the margin. The word means *to murmur (in pleasure or anger), to ponder, or to imagine*.[2]

Moses, Joshua's predecessor, was leaving. He would not be on earth much longer to coach Joshua in his new and overwhelming position. After 40 years Moses knew the job well—so well, in fact, that he understood the spiritual stamina needed to be a successful leader. Moses was saying: "Joshua, day and night you must read, ponder, and apply God's Word. You must get continual guidance from your Boss, the God of the universe."

Another classic passage using *hagah* is Psalm 1:2-3.

Understand the perimeter of Psalm 1:2-3 by reading all of Psalm 1 and writing a summary sentence here.

_____

_____

_____

A second Hebrew word translated *meditate* is *sîyach*, meaning *to ponder, to converse with oneself, to muse, or to pray*.[3] The word is first used in Psalm 119:15. Read that verse in the margin.

Other synonyms for *meditate* are *think, commune, consider,* and *remember*. Mary, Jesus' mother, is particularly noted in Scripture for her thoughtful meditation on God's Word and ways: "Mary treasured

This book of the law shall not depart from your mouth, but you shall meditate on it day and night, so that you may be careful to do according to all that is written in it; for then you will make your way prosperous, and then you will have success (Josh. 1:8).

I will meditate on Thy precepts, And regard Thy ways (Ps. 119:15).

up all these things, pondering them in her heart" (Luke 2:19).

Andrew Murray, a missionary-pastor and the writer of more than 20 devotional books, says that a primary goal of meditation is nourishing the heart: "It is in meditation that the heart holds and appropriates the Word. … The intellect gathers and prepares the food upon which we are to feed. In meditation the heart takes it in and feeds on it."[4]

Step 2: Paraphrase the Verse

Let's learn and practice the next meditation step. After understanding the verse's context, the perimeter, we need to paraphrase it. In this step God plugs His Word into the socket of your life. *Paraphrase* means *to put in your own words*. Say it; then write it down. Try to keep the paraphrase about the same number of lines as the version in your Bible.

> Yesterday we applied meditation step 1 to 1 Peter 5:7. **Today let's apply step 2. In the margin rewrite 1 Peter 5:7 in your own words.**

I wrote 1 Peter 5:7 in my heart-language: "Give every problem to God. He loves you and will carry every load." Each person's paraphrase will be different. You can receive great insights as you and your friends or group members share your paraphrases.

> **Practice paraphrasing verses. Write in your own words the verses you have memorized so far in this course.**

Jeremiah 15:16: _____

_____

Philippians 4:13: _____

_____

John 16:24: _____

_____

> **Close today's study by offering to God as a prayer one of the verses you paraphrased.**

Try to keep the paraphrase about the same number of lines as the version in your Bible.

---

[1]John Hunter, *Knowing God's Secrets* (Grand Rapids: Zondervan, 1965), 107.
[2]James Strong, *The Exhaustive Concordance of the Bible* (Hendersonville, Tenn.: Mendenhall Sales, n.d.), 82.
[3]Ibid., 115.
[4]Andrew Murray, as quoted by Wilbur M. Smith, *Profitable Bible Study*, 2nd rev. ed. (Natick, Mass.: W. A. Wilde Co., 1963), 63.

Day 3
The Process of Pulverizing

ultiple blessings are gained from Scripture meditation. Let's look at three significant ones.

Feeding the Soul

One of God's unusual men of faith was George Müller, who lived in England during the 1800s. Müller believed that God would lead hundreds of lost souls to Christ. Furthermore, without publicizing his needs, Müller prayed for money to feed over three thousand orphans in homes operated by his ministry. Over a period of 40 years and without a public request for help, God led people to send millions of dollars in response to Müller's believing prayer.

Entries in George Müller's diary, dated May 9, 1841, emphasize a breakthrough he experienced through Scripture meditation:

> *It has pleased the Lord to teach me a truth, the benefit of which I have not lost for more than fourteen years. The point is this: I saw more clearly than ever that the first great primary business to which I ought to attend every day was, to have my soul happy in the Lord ... not how much I might serve the Lord, ... but how I might get my soul into a happy state, and how my inner man might be nourished. For I might seek to set the truth before the unconverted, I might seek to benefit believers ... and yet, not being happy in the Lord, and not being nourished and strengthened in my inner man day by day, all this might not be attended to in a right spirit. Before this time my practice had been ... to give myself to prayer after having dressed myself in the morning. Now, I saw that the most important thing I had to do was to give myself to the reading of the Word of God, and to meditation on it, that thus my heart might be comforted, encouraged, warned, reproved, instructed; and that thus, by means of the Word of God, whilst meditating on it, my heart might be brought into experimental communion with the Lord.*[1]

> ✿ **Underline in the previous paragraph the primary reason George Müller meditated on God's Word.**

Müller meditated in order to have a happy, well-fed soul.

Comforting the Soul

David, the shepherd-king, punctuated his songs with insights about

---

meditation's power over pain, crisis, and insecurity. Meditate on God's Word—
❑ when facing opposition (see Ps. 119:42,97-98);
❑ when dealing with oppression (see Ps. 119:78);
❑ in times of crisis (see Ps. 119:23,148);
❑ to win over depression (see Ps. 77:11-12);
❑ when seeking God's will (see Ps. 119:10,15);
❑ to boost confidence (see Ps. 63:5-11);
❑ when longing to please God (see Ps. 19:14; 104:34).

Check the category above that best describes your most recent experience. Read the suggested passage listed. Paraphrase the verses below.

_____

_____

Providing Spiritual Success

A further great value is found in the discipline of meditation. Prosperity and success are God's promised rewards (see Josh. 1:8; Ps. 1:2-3; 1 Tim. 4:15). Notice this promise spelled out in Joshua 1:8: " 'Meditate on it day and night, ... for then you will make your way prosperous, and then you will have success.' " Successful people are those who learn to apply God's wondrous wisdom.

Meditation will greatly benefit your life. Complete the following three blessings I have presented.
1. _____ **the soul**
2. _____ **the soul**
3. **Providing spiritual** _____

Step 3: Pulverize the Verse

We've gone from understanding the perimeter (the larger context) of the verse to paraphrasing the verse. The next step is to pulverize the verse, looking at its individual words. Pulverizing involves a threefold process:
1. *Say the verse aloud.* First say the entire verse aloud to yourself. Emphasize a different word each time you slowly quote it.

Quote 1 Peter 5:7 from memory. Say it thoughtfully, emphasizing a different word each time you quote the verse. For example: "*Casting* all your anxiety upon Him, because He cares for you." Then "Casting *all* your anxiety upon Him," and so on.

> Successful people are those who learn to apply God's wondrous wisdom.

Notice the relationship of each word to the other words and to the verse's entirety. Each word has the value of a pearl in an expensive necklace. You're looking at a string of pearls, one precious pearl at a time. See how each pearl (word) adds beauty and symmetry to the whole necklace (verse).

Listen to God's Word as you read or quote it. When God speaks and we listen, He has our hearts. Action follows as we do His will and tell others about our experiences with Him.

2. *Choose one or two key words.* Three or four words may be significant in the verse, but choose the one or two that seem most important to you.

Write two words in 1 Peter 5:7 that seem most important to you.

1. _____

2. _____

Significant word-ideas I identified in 1 Peter 5:7 are *casting* and *cares.* Your goal is to discover God's will for you about the truth of the verse. Like a medical doctor who doesn't give everyone in the waiting room the same pill, the Holy Spirit leads different people to choose from a number of key words in each verse.

3. *Ask questions about one of the key words.* Think of the way a cow chews its cud. Up from its first stomach comes the partly digested food to be chewed again. Meditating on Scripture allows you to chew the meat and bread of the Word, digesting it into spiritual muscle and power. The Word becomes flesh (see John 1:14)! By asking questions, you chew an idea over and over to get maximal benefit from it.

In this final step you bombard the key word or words with questions that cry out for answers. Make these six penetrating words your friends for all methods of Bible study: *who, what, when, where, why,* and *how.* Sometimes the answer to your posed question is not in the verse or even in the chapter. That's no problem. Search other Scriptures for answers.

Select one of the two significant words you chose in 1 Peter 5:7. Write it below and develop as many questions as you can, using the following six words.

Word: _____
Who? _____
What? _____
When? _____

> **Your goal is to discover God's will for you about the truth of the verse.**

Where? _____
Why? _____
How? _____

The key word I chose in 1 Peter 5:7 was *casting*. I put it through this filtering-question process: On whom am I to cast? What does it mean to cast? When am I to cast away my anxieties? Where am I to cast? Why cast? How do I cast?

A Chinese proverb says, "When the pupil is ready, the teacher will come." Asking questions gets you ready to want an answer. The process of questioning generates a seeking heart. The right questions can penetrate your foggy familiarity with certain passages and stories from the Bible. Realizing how little you know is humbling, and asking questions reveals the depth of your emptiness. The Holy Spirit will implant new insights and joyous opportunities to make the verse live in you!

Furthermore, asking questions is an indispensable key to learning. With men I mentor, I sometimes suggest that they write 25 questions about a verse before our next time together. Then we discuss the verse in light of their questions. Illumination begins.

Meditation takes what may look like a simple picnic lunch and reveals the multiple courses of an extravagant banquet. Appetizers, soups, salads, breads, vegetables, steak, poultry, fish, and desserts appear from the picnic basket of a single verse. What a feast!

> **Memorize Psalm 1:2-3, using the process you learned last week. Use the verses printed on page 39 from the *New American Standard Bible* or choose another translation.**

> **Close today's study in prayer, asking God to open your mind and heart to receive the riches of His Word.**

> **Asking questions gets you ready to want an answer.**

---

[1]George Müller, as quoted by Wilbur M. Smith, *Profitable Bible Study*, 2nd rev. ed. (Natick, Mass.: W. A. Wilde Co., 1963), 64.

Day 4
Glue the Promise to the Problem

*T*oday we will learn another important step in meditation.

Step 4: Personalize the Verse
The fourth meditation step is to personalize the verse. Pray for wisdom

to make it flesh and blood. The goal of all study is application. Don't stop with a nice idea or an interesting concept. Activate the idea!

🌿 **One of the toughest questions I asked in step 3 about the word *casting* was "How do I cast my cares on the Lord?" Have you ever tried to give a problem to God, but it came back like a boomerang or a yo-yo? In prayer I've thrown my burden onto the Lord, and it returned in 15 minutes! How is it possible to break the cycle of worry? Answer below.**

_____

_____

God will relate a specific promise from His Word to the anxiety you're facing.

Let me tell you what I've discovered: Ask God to show you a promise from Scripture about that burden. God will relate a specific promise from His Word to the anxiety you're facing. It may take time, but God will show you. After He shows you His Word, link your burden to the Father's love and faithfulness. Claim the verse by faith. Every time the anxiety comes, reaffirm His promise by praying the verse. Think of this process as carpenter's glue. Glue the promise to the problem! Say it aloud: glue the promise to the problem. Believing the verse the Lord gives you will literally overwhelm the problem with that promise.

I remember when I felt overwhelmed—with a problem, not a promise! Getting off the plane after burying my mother, I was told that my wife's surgery for a benign tumor was more complicated than expected: cancer! A flood of fearful thoughts rushed in. I had just lost my precious mom. Now would I lose the dearest person on earth to me?

In Clemmie's hospital room the Lord whispered: "I love and care for Clemmie. Give her to Me." Through my tears I fought to place her in God's loving hands. God met us powerfully in the weeks of pain and healing that followed. Within a 20-year span Clemmie had two more cancer surgeries. We've claimed the Word, and by faith we've grasped God's strong hands as He has affirmed, " 'I have loved you with an everlasting love' " (Jer. 31:3). We've cast ourselves on Him.

🌿 **The promise in 1 Peter 5:7 is "He cares for you." What need in your life is God speaking to? Make a plan to live this Scripture in a specific way this week as you glue this verse to one anxiety (person, problem, or pressure). Write your plan in the margin.**

🌿 **End today's lesson by using meditation steps 2, 3, and 4 to meditate on Psalm 1:2-3. Allow 10 to 20 minutes for your meditation.**

Day 5
Put Yourself in the Verse

*L*et's review the first four steps in meditation.

Complete the following.
Step 1: Understand the p_____ of the verse.
Step 2: P_____ the verse.
Step 3: P_____ the verse.
Step 4: P_____ the verse.

Let's add the fifth and final step and then practice the entire process.

Step 5: Pray the Verse into Your Life

The fifth step is to pray the verse back to God, putting your name and circumstance in the verse. For example, when Clemmie was diagnosed with cancer, I prayed: "Father, thank You for wanting to carry my load. By faith, not feeling, I now give Clemmie and her cancer to You. Please carry her as You promised. I know that You care for her and for me as my heart is breaking. Thank You for holding Clemmie in Your strong hands." Satan is the great discourager. The Holy Spirit is the great encourager; His burden is light.

Put your name and circumstance in the verse.

The worksheet on page 50 directs you through the process of meditation you have learned this week. Make copies of the worksheet to use in future times of meditation. Now practice by choosing one or more of the following passages and completing the worksheet on page 50.
• **Psalm 23:1**   • **Philippians 4:13**
• **1 Thessalonians 5:21-22** • **Hebrews 13:8**

Meditation, then, is reflective thinking on God's Word and ways, with a view to application. Through this discipline you align your life with God's will and purpose as you seek to become a mature follower of Jesus Christ.

Say aloud your memory verses for this week, 1 Peter 5:7 and Psalm 1:2-3.

Close this week's study with a prayer in which you commit to grow in the discipline of meditation.

The Meditation Process

Scripture reference: _____

Step 1: Understand the perimeter of the verse:

_____

_____

Step 2: Paraphrase the verse:

_____

_____

Step 3: Pulverize the verse:
Emphasize a different word in separate readings. Choose one word that is key to the message of the verse for you.

_____

Ask questions about the word and answer them if you can:

Who? _____

What? _____

When? _____

Where? _____

Why? _____

How? _____

Step 4: Personalize the verse:
Apply the verse. Glue the promise to a problem.

_____

Step 5: Pray the verse into your life:
Ask God to make the verse a reality in your life today.

Week 4
The Time of Your Life

Day 1
Tourist or Worshiper?

Clemmie and I have traveled to London several times, where one of our favorite places to visit is Westminster Abbey. I remember one Sunday afternoon walking through crowds of tourists with their backpacks, cameras, and excited voices. We made our way to the middle side of the church for Evensong service but were stopped by a roped barricade. A distinguished man in a long black coat and white gloves stood in the aisle.

"Tourists or worshipers?" he asked. "Worshipers," we replied, smiling. He unclipped the rope, and another man ushered us to the choir loft. Our answer determined where we spent the next hour—with curious photo snappers in the back or in worship near the altar, surrounded by music.

Are you a tourist or a worshiper? I believe that your richest opportunities for living God's Word will come from daily, one-to-one worship with God as you bring Him your hungry heart. As salt is to flavor and light is to color, ultimately every area of my life has been affected by my quiet time with God. Asking Clemmie to marry me, God's call to the ministry, a surprise move to a church in Florida—every decision has been fueled by my daily time with God. I've ministered in more than 70 countries. It's no coincidence that over the past 35 years I've prayed daily that God would send laborers to every country and that I've asked God to use me through giving, training others, or going myself.

Whether you refer to your meeting with God as your quiet time, devotions, or time with God, it involves two key elements: listening to God (through His Word) and talking to God (in prayer). Like being thrilled with an adventurous vacation or a spectacular evening, you'll begin to think of being with God as the time of your life.

🌿 **Begin this week by evaluating your time with God.**
How regular is your quiet time with God?
❑ **daily**   ❑ **two or three times a week**
❑ **three or four times a month**
How much time do you spend with God in each period?
❑ **15–20 minutes** ❑ **30–45 minutes** ❑ **60 minutes or more**

THIS WEEK'S LESSONS
Day 1: Tourist or Worshiper?
Day 2: The Rewards of Time
     with God
Day 3: Daniel's Powerful
     Appointment
Day 4: God Waits Until You
     Pray
Day 5: Believing Prayer

FOCUS
This week you will consider the importance of a daily quiet time with God and will develop this discipline in your life.

MEMORY VERSES
"An hour is coming, and now is, when the true worshipers shall worship the Father in spirit and truth; for such people the Father seeks to be His worshipers" (John 4:23).

*Let me hear Thy lovingkindness
     in the morning;
For I trust in Thee;
Teach me the way in which
     I should walk;
For to Thee I lift up my soul*
     (Ps. 143:8).

When do you have your quiet time with God?

❏ morning ❏ during the day ❏ evening

What do you do when you spend time with God? Check all that apply.

❏ read the Bible ❏ meditate

❏ memorize Scripture ❏ pray

How satisfied are you with your quiet time with God?

❏ the time of my life ❏ OK ❏ needs work

Why spend time with God? Let me share three basic reasons.

Have Fellowship with the Father

The distance between God and humans is infinite. God, in His transcendent might and glorious perfection, is so far beyond us that words cannot describe the gap. However, to bridge that gap, God sacrificed His only Son, Jesus, because He values us so much.

The most exciting reason to spend time with the Father is the extraordinary fact that He wants fellowship with you. Read the apostle Paul's words in the margin. Jesus demonstrated the Father's desire for communion with us by relating to an immoral woman whom others considered untouchable. Jesus revealed a deep truth to her when she was neither right with God nor religious (see John 4)!

The Samaritans were Jews who had intermarried with Gentiles. They wrongly resisted going to the temple in Jerusalem to worship. They wanted worship on their own terms in their own province. Jesus told the woman at the well that the most important issue in worship is your heart, not a building. Christianity is a relationship with One we know, not somewhere we go.

A worshiping heart that follows God's truth has an instant-access button. You don't have to find God. God has a passion for fellowship, and He's seeking you.

God is faithful, through whom you were called into fellowship with His Son, Jesus Christ our Lord (1 Cor. 1:9).

🌿 Read John 4:23 as quoted on page 51 from the *New American Standard Bible* or read the verse from another translation. Begin memorizing it, using the process you learned in week 2.

Prepare for the Day

Can you imagine going to work day after day without consulting your boss to get direction? Another reason to have a quiet time is to get orders for the day from your Boss and the Captain of your salvation.

*Let me hear Thy lovingkindness
in the morning;
For I trust in Thee;
Teach me the way in which
I should walk;
For to Thee I lift up my soul
(Ps. 143:8).*

🌿 Another verse you will memorize later this week is Psalm 143:8. Read it in the margin. What time of day does the writer of the psalm meet with God? _____

Ideally, in the morning you need to focus on God's order in the seeming chaos of life. You need preparation for what is ahead—possible detours, surprises, or roadblocks. Read Psalm 37:31 in the margin. The Lord prepares you for these events through your quiet time.

The law of his God is in his heart;
His steps do not slip (Ps. 37:31).

Read **Psalm 5:3 in the margin. If you do not have an established time of day for your quiet time, consider the morning. Read the following Scripture passages and identify the persons who rose early to be with God.**
Genesis 19:27: _____ rose early to meet the Lord.
Exodus 34:4: _____ rose early to meet God at Sinai.
Job 1:5: _____ rose early to offer sacrifices.
Mark 1:35: _____ rose early to pray in a quiet place.
Luke 21:38: The _____ rose early to hear Jesus.
Mark 16:2: The _____ rose early to go to the tomb.

In the morning, O Lord, you hear
my voice;
in the morning I lay my
requests before you
and wait in expectation
(Ps. 5:3, NIV).

God Shapes Your Life

H. J. Taylor was a salesman who became a merchandising multimillionaire with his company, Club Aluminum. God chose to trust him with unusual financial success. I heard him speak at a retreat about the main lesson he had learned in life: he had made daily time with God a priority. This time with God shaped his marriage, his business, and his employees.

H. J. Taylor amazed the two hundred listeners by quoting Matthew 5 from the Sermon on the Mount. He smiled. "For years since I discovered the imperative need for daily time with God, I memorized and have quoted Matthew 5—7 each day before work." That's over one hundred verses! From Jesus' sermon God revealed to Taylor four business principles for treating others fairly. This is Taylor's four-way test of the things we think, say, or do:
1. Is it the truth?
2. Is it fair to all concerned?
3. Will it build good will and better friendships?
4. Will it be beneficial to all concerned?

The Father desires fellowship with us. We gain preparation for the day when we spend time with God. God shapes our lives through regular quiet times with Him. The question "Tourists or worshipers?" describes the decision you make each day about relating to your Father. God beckons you to sit at His feet each day and be a worshiper.

During your quiet time today, apply the process *know, stop, change, start,* which you learned in week 1, to Matthew 7:21-29.

Day 2
The Rewards of Time with God

*T*oday we will consider several benefits you will receive from having a regular quiet time. First recall what the verse you memorized yesterday says about your time with God.

In the margin write John 4:23 from memory. Meditate on this verse, using the steps you learned last week.

Reward 1: Reaping a Life for God

We love the finished product: the playing of a virtuoso, the beauty of a painting, the furniture built by a master cabinetmaker. People don't begin playing music, painting, or woodworking perfectly. They must sow in practice to reap in production and brilliance.

You may think, *I want God to use me now,* but you haven't paid the price of meeting with God day after day. The hours you spend alone with God will produce fruit now but much more at a later time. There is no shortcut to spiritual maturity. The disciples and Paul sowed years of their lives in getting to know Christ. They reaped the writing of the New Testament and the planting of a worldwide church.

Though the field of your life may lie fallow for a season, God never wastes the time you spend learning or the months you're in the deserts of life. Start where you are. Sow the seed of the Word through Scripture memorization, meditation, and immersing your heart in His. Read God's promise in Galatians 6:7,9, which appears in the margin. Notice the harvest principles in this passage:

- You reap what you sow.
- You reap more than you sow, because the seed multiplies.
- You reap in proportion to what you sow—sow a little, reap a little; sow a lot, reap a lot.
- You will eventually reap unless you lose heart in the field.

My mentor, Dawson Trotman, once challenged me to meditate on 1 Corinthians 10:13: "God is faithful, who will not allow you to be tempted beyond what you are able." I meditated on it in my quiet time. Two days later I was a decision counselor at an altar call. The man I spoke with was under conviction and wanted to be saved. But he remarked: "I can't live that kind of life. I have no power." First Corinthians 10:13 was the exact verse to meet his problem. When I shared it, he gave his life to Christ. What God had sown in my heart reaped a life for Him.

Reward 2: Knowing and Loving God

Time with God is essential to knowing God. To know God is to grow to

Do not be deceived, God is not mocked; for whatever a man sows, this he will also reap. Let us not lose heart in doing good, for in due time we shall reap if we do not grow weary (Gal. 6:7,9).

love Him. Courtship and marriage are only the beginning of the process of knowing another person. One joy of marriage is delight in knowing your spouse and growing in that knowledge. Paul had as his goal "that I may know Him, and the power of His resurrection and the fellowship of His sufferings" (Phil. 3:10). The process of knowing and experiencing God deepens in proportion to the time we spend with Him in the Word and prayer.

In the Philippines a few years ago I was on the island of Mindinao under a heavy load of preaching. I'd been traveling across those beautiful islands without word from Clemmie in two weeks. The open-sided auditorium was hot and humid. Two language groups were present in the meetings, so I repeatedly had to stop for the interpreters.

Just before I preached the evening message, a missionary handed me a letter from Clemmie. When do you think I opened it? The moment after I'd preached and the benediction was given? The next day? Neither! That minute I ripped open the letter and read the last line on the last page—to see that she still loved me after two weeks!

I couldn't wait to read Clemmie's letter, because I'm in love with her. The Bible is God's love letter to you. How many days do you wait to read the Father's love letter to you? God is telling you that He loves you. He wants you to experience His great love and plan.

> The process of knowing and experiencing God deepens in proportion to the time we spend with Him in the Word and prayer.

Reward 3: Becoming like Christ

Jesus modeled for us His total dependence on His Father through His prayer life. Jesus prayed alone (see Mark 1:35; Luke 4:42). He prayed at His baptism (see Luke 3:21). Jesus cried out to God all night before choosing the twelve (see Luke 6:12). He prayed before performing miracles and while hanging on the cross (see Luke 9:16; 23:34,46). "During the days of Jesus' life on earth, he offered up prayers and petitions with loud cries and tears to the one who could save him from death, and he was heard because of his reverent submission" (Heb. 5:7, NIV). Throughout Scripture our Lord teaches us critical principles for effective answers to prayer:

- Ask in His name
- Ask with sin confessed
- Ask according to God's will
- Ask by faith
- Ask persistently
- Ask in the Spirit

We become like Jesus when we spend time with Him daily.

Reward 4: Being Empowered for Daily Living

Giving up and bailing out are epidemic in Christians' lives. According to Jesus, one source of discouragement is missing regular time with the living God. Jesus encouraged His disciples " 'that at all times they ought to pray and not to lose heart' " (Luke 18:1). Another version translates this: " 'pray and not give up' " (NIV). Do you feel dry and empty in your walk with God? If you don't have a strong habit of prayer, you'll run out of spiritual gas. If you're not in the Word, you will slide into mediocrity and then ruin. Spending time with God empowers you for daily living.

To energize a passage during your time with God, use all of your senses to focus on the person of Christ. Read Matthew 9:27-38 in your Bible. Check each item below as you complete it.

❑ Meditate on the ideas.

❑ Color the passage with your senses: what do you see, hear, taste, touch, and smell?

❑ Give the scene structure, fabric, time, faces, and action. Listen to the moment.

❑ Discover one quality, characteristic, or facet of Jesus' personality you can thank Him for now. Soak up the experience with Jesus.

❑ Imagine that you're someone in the event. How do you feel? What response should you make?

❑ As the Spirit leads you, tell the Lord of your love. Surrender yourself anew to Christ Himself. Worship Him.

Day 3
Daniel's Powerful Appointment

*D*aniel was a prophet of God, an adviser to the king of the Babylonians, one of the most powerful men who has ever lived. God gave Daniel supernatural insights into the future that He trusted to no other person. The Book of Daniel reveals again and again that Daniel spent time meditating on the Word and waiting in God's presence.

You are probably familiar with the account of Daniel in the lions' den. Prior to this punishment a 30-day law had promised the death penalty for anyone who prayed to someone other than the king. Even the sentence of death, however, couldn't stop Daniel from keeping this daily appointment with God. Read Daniel 6:10 in the margin. Daniel sought the God he had known intimately for years.

But Daniel's enemies set him up to be arrested: "Then these men came by agreement and found Daniel making petition and supplication before his God" (Dan. 6:11). Though the king was bound by his own law, God had the last word: He dramatically rescued Daniel from the lions. Let's learn from Daniel the elements of spending time with God that enabled him to stand in the center of God's loving, powerful will.

Now when Daniel knew that the document was signed, he entered his house (now in his roof chamber he had windows open toward Jerusalem); and he continued kneeling on his knees three times a day, praying and giving thanks before his God, as he had been doing previously (Dan. 6:10).

A Place for Time with God

Daniel went into his house to a particular room where he could concentrate. Jesus called this place your closet, or "inner room." Read His instruction about it in the margin.

I know a successful businessman who built a prayer closet in his house, complete with light, air conditioning, a chair, a kneeling rail, a table, and a bookshelf. I've tried all sorts of ways to be alone with God. I've sneaked away from my children and sat in my car in the garage. I've walked through the streets of our neighborhood reading my Bible and praising God.

The inner room of Suzanna Wesley was unusual. She lived in London during the 18th century, a stay-at-home mom with 11 children. When she wanted private time with the Lord, Suzanna would put an apron or a cloth over her head. That was a signal to John, Charles, and the other kids to play quietly. Suzanna is a terrific example that you can pray anywhere anytime.

The best place to pray is where you can pray aloud. When you pray aloud, you can respond emotionally. You will have added joy and exuberance when you talk with the Father just as you would to a friend. You'll discover that praying aloud is radically different from praying silently. It could revolutionize your prayer life.

"You, when you pray, go into your inner room, and when you have shut your door, pray to your Father who is in secret, and your Father who sees in secret will repay you" (Matt. 6:6).

Identify your place for time with God. Before you write it, evaluate the place you select. Does it provide the best environment for you to be alone with God? My place for time with God: _____

A Time to Meet with God

Can you pray anytime? Absolutely. In the Bible we read about people who prayed on many different occasions. As we noted yesterday, Jesus prayed at various times and on many occasions. On the other hand, you will find great success in meeting God before you step into the activities of your day. Our Lord indicated by example that a favorite prayer time was first thing in the morning. Read Mark 1:35 in the margin.

Jesus routinely spent time with His Father before dawn. As fully God and fully man, He faced the same temptations and discouragements you and I do. Jesus needed His sleep, too. However, Jesus knew how critical this preparation was to the remainder of His waking hours.

When I lived in Boston, I had decided to meet the Lord in the mornings, but the winters were very cold, and the house thermometer was set very low. I decided to pray in bed, where it was warm. Soon I was "meditating" with my eyes closed! Someone who was more accustomed to cold winters gave me a verse that convicted me: "The sluggard will not plow by reason of the cold; therefore shall he beg in harvest, and have nothing" (Prov. 20:4, KJV).

In the early morning, while it was still dark, He arose and went out and departed to a lonely place, and was praying there (Mark 1:35).

The criterion for choosing a time is to give God your best time for prayer and Bible study, whenever that is.

For victory in meeting God, make an appointment the night before. I spell *appointment* A-L-A-R-M C-L-O-C-K!

The criterion for choosing a time is to give God your best time for prayer and Bible study, whenever that is. Some people get up later because they stay up later. My son, a single adult, prefers to pray late in the evenings, sometimes after midnight. Whatever works best for you, select a time and keep your appointment with God.

Identify your best time to be alone with God. Write it below. Make a commitment to keep it for two weeks. After two weeks, evaluate it and make adjustments if needed. My time to be alone with God: _____ ❑ a.m. ❑ p.m.

A Plan for Time with God

You have a place and a period to spend time with God. Next, decide what type of study plan you will use. Scheduling this ahead of time saves you from fumbling through the Bible in pursuit of a passage to read or from searching for your prayer list or journal.

Whatever plan you use, make a habit to record what God says to you. Write in a journal what you're learning. List prayer requests and answers from the Lord in your computer files. Type or write down meaningful Scriptures that are relevant to your life situation. These journals, notebooks, and files may become the most treasured books in your home, as they are in ours. Purchase a journal or follow the format on page 21 to write journal entries in a notebook.

Adjust your program or plan to your own personality and style. I get bored easily, so I often vary my plan to include different elements of studying the Word and prayer. The following examples are some methods I've used.

The Word	Prayer
• Meditate on a verse you've been memorizing.	• Begin a prayer list, recording requests and answers to prayer.
• Read the proverb corresponding to today's date (March 17 = Prov. 3:17).	• Pray a passage back to God.
• Look for specific items in a passage: a sin to confess, a promise to claim, a blessing to praise God for, a command to obey, a trait of Jesus or God.	• Spend five minutes in each element of prayer: praise, confession, singing, thanksgiving, intercession, listening, and petition.

There is no substitute for a quiet time with God. Any lasting impact you make for God's glory grows from your daily relationship with your Lord. Schedules and to-do lists, our personal drives, and the environment of our world encourage us either to trivialize God or to substitute other things for Him. Temptations to squeeze God out may come from good things such as Christian service, family demands, people's needs, and even sleep. Unfortunately, these may become substitutes for knowing and experiencing God.

🌿 **Identify your plan for time alone with God. Choose a plan and try it for two weeks before you make a change. Briefly describe your plan below.**

_____

_____

Who you are in Christ is more important than what you do for Christ. Being is the basis for doing. Oswald Chambers wrote: "Christian service is not our work; loyalty to Jesus is our work."[1] "We are saved and sanctified not for service, but to be absolutely Jesus Christ's, the consuming passion of the life is for Him."[2]

🌿 **Memorize Psalm 143:8, using the process you learned in week 2. You may choose to memorize the verse on page 51 from the *New American Standard Bible* or to use another translation.**

🌿 **Close today's study in prayer. Make a commitment to be faithful in meeting with God at the time and place you have chosen.**

---

[1] Oswald Chambers, *Disciples Indeed* (Fort Washington, Penn.: Christian Literature Crusade, 1995), 85.
[2] Ibid., 61.

Any lasting impact you make for God's glory grows from your daily relationship with your Lord.

Day 4
God Waits Until You Pray

Prayer and the Word are the ingredients of your time with God. We have discussed how important God's Word is, and we have developed skills to help us internalize His Word. Today and tomorrow we will look at two foundational prayer principles. Both principles relate to acting on God's promises as given in Scripture.

We are God's fellow workers; you are God's field, God's building (1 Cor. 3:9).

Principle 1: We Limit God When We Don't Pray

Great revivalists of past centuries had a startling insight into prayer: God waits to act until you pray. John Wesley said, "God will do nothing but in answer to prayer." What a profound statement! On one hand, God is sovereign. On the other hand, His goodness, grace, and power can be blocked from our lives because we do not pray. God chooses to let us labor with Him (see 1 Cor. 3:9 in the margin). Therefore, by failing to pray according to His will and Word, we can "tie His hands." Let's look at some passages that underline this teaching.

Israel was in bondage 30 years too long. God blessed Abram with good news: he would become the father of the Israelites. But God also told him about Israel's troubled future. God's people would be held in captivity for 400 years (see Gen. 15:13). However, Exodus 12:40 states that Israel was captive in Egypt for 430 years. Why the 30-year discrepancy? Israel was a slave race in Egypt who did not turn to God in their troubles. Their griping was not praying. Their heartless worship was not praying. God waited for them to pray and believe Him. His promises are true, but they wait to be claimed.

While waiting, God was preparing Moses, an Israelite who'd been trained for leadership in Pharaoh's palace. God, however, had another level of leadership for Moses to learn. Moses tended sheep in the Midian desert 30 years longer than God's promise because the people didn't pray. When they began to pray, God immediately called Moses to lead them to freedom: " 'Now, behold, the cry of the sons of Israel has come to Me; … I will send you to Pharaoh, so that you may bring My people, the sons of Israel, out of Egypt' " (Ex. 3:9-10). Until Israel prayed, one of the greatest leaders of all time was tending sheep!

Worth remembering: God's _____ are true, but they _____ to be claimed.

Israel discovered where the real battle is won. God's blessings come when His people really pray. Israel fought a life-or-death battle against the nation of Amalek (see Ex. 17:8-16). Joshua was in a valley leading the soldiers of Israel while Moses stationed himself on top of the hill. With the staff of God in his hands, Moses stood with hands lifted in prayer, as was his custom. When Moses' hands were up, Israel won. When Moses got tired, his prayers stopped, and Amalek won. Lives were lost when Moses stopped interceding.

Aaron and Hur saw the battle turn from victory to defeat when Moses got tired. Quickly they found a stone for Moses to sit on. Then each grabbed one of Moses' hands and lifted it high. These two men held up Moses' arms for hours. Joshua's men overwhelmed the Amalekite army. Moses built a memorial altar, calling it *The Lord is my Banner, Jehovah-Nissi.* Here is an astounding principle: The battle had to be fought man against man in the valley. But the battle was actually won through intercession on the mountain.

🌿 **Worth *remembering*: God's _____ come when His people really _____.**

God looked in vain for an intercessor. An intercessor stands between God and others to bring the two together. The prophet Ezekiel recorded God's anger and coming vengeance on apostate, filthy Israel. Then God made a strange, pleading statement: " 'I looked for a man among them who would build up the wall and stand before me in the gap on behalf of the land so I would not have to destroy it, but I found none' " (Ezek. 22:30, NIV). He wanted someone with courage and commitment to stand between His just wrath and His unlimited grace. The way this person would stand in the gap was through prayer, pulling God's abundant grace into the vortex of judgment against Israel.

Religious people were everywhere, but no intercessor was found. Verse 31 gives us the tragic conclusion: God poured out His judgment, consuming them with the fire of His wrath, for lack of someone to pray. Is anyone in your family really praying? Are you? Who is standing between God and His judgment on the sins of your nation, your children, or your church? How thankful we are for Jesus, who "always lives to make intercession" for us (Heb. 7:25). Yet amazingly, God has chosen us to be His heart and voice on earth, to bring life through prayer.

🌿 **Worth *remembering*: God pours out His _____ for lack of someone to _____.**

Josiah led the people to repent. Josiah, who ruled Judah for 31 years, was a godly king. He put an end to idol worship and began to repair the temple in Jerusalem. There Hilkiah the priest discovered the book of the law, our Book of Deuteronomy, which had called Israel to exclusive loyalty to God. When Josiah heard the law read, he tore his clothes in repentance, realizing that God would punish His people because they had not kept His covenant. Because Josiah humbled Himself before God, God promised to delay Israel's punishment until after Josiah's death (see 2 Chron. 34:14-28).

Josiah read God's Word to the people and led them to repent. They renewed their covenant relationship with God and pledged to keep His commands. God withheld His judgment from that generation. God's mercy awaits those who repent.

🌿 **Worth *remembering*: God's _____ awaits those who _____.**

> Amazingly, God has chosen us to be His heart and voice on earth, to bring life through prayer.

Promises claimed—nations won to Christ. Scripture is the other building block of the devotional life. Saul was a fervent, educated rabbi who called himself a "Hebrew of Hebrews" and kept to the Pharisees' letter of the law (see Phil. 3:5). What a career change he later undertook! He changed his name, using a Greek name, Paul, and devoted his life to witnessing to the Gentiles after God revealed amazing promises to him.

His Jewish nation had never fulfilled God's original calling: to be evangelists to reach the world. As Paul read the Scriptures, God opened his eyes to verses indicating that pagan Gentiles were ready and willing to be saved. The harvest was white, but not a single laborer would answer the call. In Romans 15:8-13 Paul summarized his discovery of God's plan that the Gentiles glorify Him. (Note the promises: v. 9 quotes Ps. 18:49; v. 10 quotes Deut. 32:43; v. 11 quotes Ps. 117:1; v. 12 quotes Isa. 11:10.)

This staggering insight refocused Saul's evangelistic target from Jews to Gentiles. Acting in faith, Paul was able to win and disciple hundreds who reached, in turn, thousands, then millions. God found someone who believed His promises, and it changed our world forever.

> **God found someone who believed His promises, and it changed our world forever.**

🌿 **Complete the first prayer principle you have learned today: We** _____ **God when we don't** _____.

🌿 **God waits until you claim His Word, His promises in prayer. What's the biggest thing you've asked God to do this year? Briefly describe it below.**

_____

_____

Ask God to direct you in this area of your life. Pray now.

Believe and claim some of the hundreds of promises in Scripture our loving Lord has for you. "By these He has granted to us His precious and magnificent promises, in order that by them you might become partakers of the divine nature" (2 Pet. 1:4). You might begin with a wonderful promise that Paul shared: "Now may the God of hope fill you with all joy and peace in believing, that you may abound in hope by the power of the Holy Spirit" (Rom. 15:13). Glue one promise to a specific need in your life this week.

🌿 **Take time to meditate on Psalm 143:8. Close today's study by repeating from memory John 4:23.**

Day 5
Believing Prayer

esterday we considered prayer principle 1: We limit God when we don't pray. Today we will consider a second principle for acting on God's promises as given in Scripture.

Principle 2: God Is Able and Ready, Waiting for Us to Believe Him

In cold, snowy Massachusetts I worked for two years on the staff of a respected college ministry. I lived with a family in a Boston suburb who helped me financially. The drawback was that it took me two hours to travel to the MIT and Harvard campuses—two hours each way. I had to walk to catch the bus. Just imagine the New England slush! Then I got on the subway, then on the elevated train, and back on the bus.

This four-hour travel schedule robbed me of needed time with the students. I prayed many times for a car to shorten my trip to 40 minutes each way. However, other than room and board, my wages were only $16 a week. There had to be a better way.

About that time a nursing student told me about an unusual and wonderful woman named Grace Tibbetts. "Aunt Tibbs" had cancer and lived in a nursing home. She had determined to make her room a prayer chapel, privately praying for everyone who entered. The nursing students opened their hearts to her, and they bought Aunt Tibbs a telephone so that people could call in requests. Aunt Tibbs prayed for anyone, day or night.

I decided to get her counsel on how to pray for a car. After listening to my frustration, Aunt Tibbs responded: "Waylon, it seems that God wants you to have an auto so that you can give more time to students and can take teams to churches. How do you pray for this?" I replied: "I've been praying: 'Lord, give me transportation. Please, Lord, I need transportation.' " She looked surprised. "Oh, is that the way you pray? I believe I understand your problem. Asking God is never enough. You must come in faith to believe God. Asking God is warming up the engine; believing God is shifting into gear! You've never thanked God by faith for the car. Faith is the doorway to receiving God's promises."

🌿 *Worth remembering:* _____ is the

doorway to receiving God's _____.

Before I left the room, Aunt Tibbs gave final instructions: "As you walk out in the snow, thank the Lord for the car He's going to give you

> **"Asking God is never enough. You must come in faith to believe God."**

and its warm heater. When you board the bus, thank the Lord for the smooth ride in your car."

Kind of an eccentric lady, I thought as I waited for the bus in the snow. When the bus came, I took a seat and looked out the window as the snow fell. "Thank You, Lord, for the warm car." I hung on to the safety strap as the subway rocked. "Thank You, Lord, for the nice smooth auto."

Meditating on Romans 4:17-21 encouraged my faith further. Abraham had received a miracle promise from God that he would be the father of a nation—although he was one hundred years old, he had no children, and his aged wife was sterile: "With respect to the promise of God, he did not waver in unbelief, but grew strong in faith, giving glory to God, and being fully assured that what He had promised, He was able also to perform" (Rom. 4:20-21). God wanted me to believe Him, my faith fueled by His promises. I was to personalize this powerful passage on faith: "God ... calls into being that which does not exist. In hope against hope he [Abraham] believed, in order that he might become a father of many nations, according to [God's promise]" (Rom. 4:17-18). I learned this in the *King James Version:* Faith "calleth those things which be not as though they were" (Rom. 4:17). Faith acts about the things that don't exist as though they did, when God's instructions say so. God was able and ready, but He was waiting for me to believe Him!

A month later I attended a student retreat, where some of the new converts through the campus ministry gave wonderful testimonies. An older man at the retreat, John Talcott, seemed quite interested in our work. He told me that he'd been praying for New England university ministry for a couple of months—the same time I'd been praying for a car! "What do you need for your ministry?" he asked. I answered vaguely, saying that we had several needs.

Then he startled me with this very direct question: "Do you need transportation?" He used the exact word I'd used in my prayers! Faith believes in God, who "calls into being that which does not exist." I enthusiastically explained how a car would greatly aid our work. Mr. Talcott smiled. "What kind of car do you need?" "I haven't prayed about that," I said, getting excited. That night I sought God in prayer. We needed a station wagon so that students could travel together and share testimonies in churches.

The next day I told Mr. Talcott that we needed a station wagon. "Do you need a used or new auto?" he asked. "I haven't prayed about that!" I responded, surprised. He asked me to research comparative prices and call him. The next week I talked with our church's car dealer. He gave me two quotes: a new station wagon at his wholesale cost and a used one that was a bit lower. When I called Mr. Talcott, he thought for a minute and then replied, "I think we should get the new one, don't

Faith acts about the things that don't exist as though they did.

you?" This was an amen moment entirely beyond any expectation! Mr. Talcott sent a check for the full amount. Faith "calleth those things which be not as though they were." What a ministry we had in the brand-new station wagon that God provided!

🌿 Principle 2: God is _____ and _____,

waiting for us to _____ Him.

🌿 Look at your prayer list. Answer the following questions.

Have you believed God about a request? ❏ Yes   ❏ No
What verse or promise has God linked to it?

_____

Search the Scriptures, seeking a word from God about your request.

🌿 If you are a parent, teach your children a new method of prayer. Start with familiar words you want your kids to use daily: "please" (intercession and petition), "thank You" (thanksgiving), "I love You" (adoration and worship), and "I'm sorry" (confession).

🌿 Put into practice what you have learned so far in *Living God's Word*. During your quiet time with God today and the next two days at (time) _____ a.m./p.m. at (place) _____, review and meditate on some of the Scriptures you have memorized so far. I suggest the following schedule. Check off each assignment as you complete it.
❏ Today: Jeremiah 15:16
❏ Tomorrow: Philippians 4:13
❏ Next day: John 16:24

🌿 Recite Psalm 143:8 from memory. Then be still and spend time with your Heavenly Father.

Search the Scriptures, seeking a word from God about your request.

Week 5
Wearing God's Names

Day 1
Try One on for Size

The living God! at his name my heart, my whole being thrills with joy" (Ps. 84:2, Knox).

FOCUS
This week you will consider the importance of names that identify and describe the Deity and will practice wearing those names.

MEMORY VERSES
From the rising of the sun
*   to its setting*
The name of the Lord is to
*   be praised (Ps. 113:3).*

A child will be born to us, a Son
*   will be given to us;*
And the government will rest on
*   His shoulders;*
And His name will be called
*   Wonderful Counselor,*
*   Mighty God,*
Eternal Father, Prince of
*   Peace (Isa. 9:6).*

In the city of Antioch the first-century believers in Jesus were first called Christians (see Acts 11:26). Little Christs, Jesus people. That title is still one way people know who we are. However, there's a more significant way people know that we belong to the Lord: Scripture commands us to clothe ourselves with the Lord Jesus (see Rom. 13:14). We clothe ourselves with Jesus through our godly attitudes and actions. Jesus' character is integrated into our lives as we experience the unusual power of knowing God's names. This week we will look at the importance God places on name giving and name wearing.

What's in a Name?
In Bible times a name summed up the character of a man or a woman. His or her name would bring to mind the whole person. The Lord attached great significance to names. Some Bible characters were given a new name when the original name was too small for God's plan. For example, *Abram*, which means *the father of many*, became *Abraham, the father of nations* (see Gen. 17:5). After his life-changing experience at Peniel, God changed Jacob's name to *Israel* (see Gen. 32:28). *Simon* means *pebble*; Jesus changed it to *Peter, the rock* (see Matt. 16:18).

A name might prophesy a parent's hopes for a child. Samson, the ultimate offensive machine and warrior for God, had a name meaning *sunlight*. However, this meaning was tragically halted by the lights-out consequence of his lust: his immoral girlfriend betrayed him to his enemies, who put out his eyes.

My name seems handpicked by God. *Waylon* means *traveler*. How appropriate for someone who has traveled to more than 70 nations!

🌿 **Do you know what your name means? Do some research this week if you don't know. My name, _____, means _____.**

God's Names

More important than God's naming people are the names He chooses to describe Himself. God uses different names to give us a complete picture of who He is and what He promises. Each name illuminates His wonder, character, actions, and will. Three names are most commonly used for God: *Jehovah* or *Yahweh* (Lord, in all capital letters, as in Gen. 2:4), *Adonai* (Lord, as in Gen. 15:2), and *Elohim* (God, as in Gen. 1:1).

Each of God's names is a photograph of His invisible essence—gift-wrapped in love and awaiting your careful observation. These pictures belong not on a table but in your heart. As you experience the pressures of the day, the picture of God from His name can fuse with an opportunity to relate to Him. Your capacity to trust the Lord is linked to a knowledge of His names and character. Read Psalm 9:10 in the margin.

One of God's names encouraged me when I was in a motel room far from home. Tired and discouraged, I wanted to be home with my family. As I read Psalm 90, the Father drew me to verse 1: "Lord, Thou hast been our dwelling place." I suddenly saw that I carry "home" wherever I go, because the Lord is my dwelling place. "Home" is a Person, not a place. When I'm in the center of God's will, I'm home—in a rental car, an airplane, or a motel. I confessed my self-pitying attitude and began to rejoice. God invited me to learn a side of Him I'd never known.

Experience the living God as you personalize one of Christ's names in your life today. First, put on the virtue. Allow the Lord to link His character trait to a need in your life.

Those who know Thy name will put their trust in Thee; For thou, O Lord, has not forsaken those who seek Thee (Ps. 9:10).

🌿 **Pray, using the name of *Shepherd* from John 10:10: Lord Jesus, You're my Shepherd today. I am Your sheep. Thank You for going ahead of me. I need Your guidance and direction about _____.**
I'm going to follow You. I will not bound ahead as sheep do. You are my protection. Remove my fears.

Next, pass on this virtue by living God's name before other people.

🌿 **Pray: Lord, thank You for being my Savior-Shepherd. Let me be like You. As Your protection and watchful eye quiet my heart, help me to pass on Your character. As a protector and shepherd, help me make others feel secure.**

A saying goes, "You may be the only Jesus someone ever sees." So show your colors! Wear Christ's names boldly. Wear them in your heart!

🌿 **Close today's study by memorizing Psalm 113:3. Use the memorization process you learned in week 2.**

Day 2
The Creative Carpenter

Help us, O God of our salvation, for the glory of Thy name;
And deliver us, and forgive our sins, for Thy name's sake (Ps. 79:9).

*M*ore than 700 names and titles of God can be found in Scripture. More than 250 of these names relate to and reveal God's Son, Jesus. Like a TV monitor using thousands of dots to show a picture, these names form a variegated array of colored dots that define our Savior and Lord Jesus. "Every name that He wears is a blessing that He shares."[1]

Jesus the Carpenter
To demonstrate how we can wear a name used to describe Jesus, let's focus on a title given to Jesus by those in His hometown of Nazareth. God had the name included in Scripture for a reason. Through it we can get very close to Jesus. In Mark 6:1-6 Jesus is called the carpenter of Nazareth. In Matthew 13:55 He is called the carpenter's son. To the villagers, Jesus was one of Joseph and Mary's children, the eldest of seven. Jesus came first as a serving carpenter, not as a king.

Why did God choose a carpenter's house for His only begotten Son? All rabbis had vocations. The apostle Paul was a tentmaker. But there was more on God's mind than making a living. It seems natural to think of Jesus in a carpenter's shop when you recall that Jesus built the universe (see Col. 1:16 and Heb. 1:2 in the margin). All things were made by Him and for Him. Jesus knew a lot about building. Jesus understood the twofold work of a carpenter: building and repairing.

Today our eternal Carpenter continues to build. Christ is building His church through our witness as people are won to faith in Him. He is also building a home in heaven for each of His own (see John 14:1-3 in the margin). Furthermore, Jesus builds lives for God's glory. The Carpenter is still working on you and me. Some doubters pull out too soon and don't wait for the Carpenter to finish. Their unbelief can split the green wood or leave unfinished the progress Jesus wants to make.

Recalling your Christian pilgrimage, briefly describe how Christ has worked to build your life for His service.

_____

_____

In Him all things were created, both in the heavens and on earth, visible and invisible, whether thrones or dominions or rulers or authorities—all things have been created through Him and for Him (Col. 1:16).

In these last days [God] has spoken to us in His Son, whom He appointed heir of all things, through whom also He made the world (Heb. 1:2).

"Let not your heart be troubled; believe in God, believe also in Me. In My Father's house are many dwelling places; if it were not so, I would have told you; for I go to prepare a place for you. And if I go and prepare a place for you, I will come again, and receive you to Myself; that where I am, there you may be also (John 14:1-3).

Carpenters not only build things of value from raw material, but they also repair broken things (see Isa. 58:12 in the margin). Have you ever been broken? All through the Bible God is depicted as the God of the needy, used, and helpless.

Our kids' grandfather used to enjoy woodworking. He made a glue from a cow's hoof that smelled worse than terrible. But this glue was necessary in repairing broken furniture. He put the hot glue on the edges of broken parts, then clamped the cracked or loose part to the larger piece. He turned the screw tightly. If wood could cry, it would have screamed, "I'm being squeezed to death!" Yet the pressure of the tightened clamp bonded that splintered wood into an amazingly whole piece, actually making the repair stronger than the original wood. Jesus repairs broken hearts, broken homes, and broken families in a similar way if we only submit to His strong, loving hands.

Describe a time when you submitted to Jesus and let Him repair brokenness in your life.

_____

_____

*"Those from among you will rebuild the ancient ruins;
You will raise up the age-old foundations;
And you will be called the repairer of the breach,
The restorer of the streets in which to dwell" (Isa. 58:12).*

Built by the Carpenter

As a child Jesus carried wood, and he grew up to cut down trees and pull logs. His hands held a saw of iron, and He learned to shape and finish wood. Carpenters of that day made chairs, tables, boxes, oxen yokes, benches, and wheels. Jesus learned the particular strengths of each type of wood: cedar, juniper, olive, fig, and sycamore. As a carpenter Jesus looked for the right greenness or dryness of the wood for the job.

Jesus our Carpenter envisions what the completed product will look like. Seeing the potential in your life, He can shape you to accomplish His will. He knows your strengths and spiritual gift(s). He saw the rock in the pebble Simon Peter. Jesus knew that a son of thunder would become John, the apostle of love. Joseph became the encourager Barnabas.

See the hands of Jesus. Gently, with calloused and splinter-embedded fingers, He healed. Jesus touched the lepers, the dead, the sick, and the sick of heart. His hands were so strong that they pulled a water-soaked Peter from the sea to walk with Him to the boat. Later those hands would be torn with Roman spikes as the Carpenter died, hanging outstretched for you on a cross.

Many African and Asian new believers choose new names to symbolize the transformation in their lives. Jesus picked you (see Eph. 1:4 in the margin), as if from a forest like an unhewn tree. Knowing your

He chose us in him before the foundation of the world, that we should be holy and blameless before Him (Eph. 1:4).

Whom He foreknew, He also pre-destined to become conformed to the image of His Son, that He might be the first-born among many brethren (Rom. 8:29).

frame, He is carefully shaping your uniqueness into His image (see Rom. 8:29 in the margin). Do you feel His hands on your life? He will never discard you. Let Him gently yet firmly perfect you and finish His task. It is awesome to be in the hands of the Master Carpenter!

 Do you see how the name *Carpenter* brings meaning to your relationship with Jesus? Does Jesus want to repair something in your life? Will you surrender to the Carpenter to do His work? Or is Jesus trying to build something new in your life? Pray to your Carpenter to begin this special work now.

 Close today's study by meditating on Psalm 113:3.

---

¹Warren Wiersbe, *The Wonderful Names of Jesus* (Lincoln, Neb.: Victor Books, 1980), 5.

Day 3
The King of Joy!

From the rising of the sun to its setting
The name of the Lord is to be praised (Ps. 113:3).

When I was a child, I had trouble relating to the Jesus I thought I knew from Sunday School. I grew up imagining Him wearing a clean, white sheet for clothes! This seemed strange to me, since only girls wore dresses. I could neither identify with his bearded face nor with His "bless you" demeanor, patting lambs and babies. Unfortunately, even into adulthood my picture of Jesus was distorted and vague. Over the years God has mightily used one of Jesus' names to radically refocus my view of Him.

The Anointed One

The kings of the earth take their stand, …
Against the Lord and against His Anointed (Ps. 2:2).

Anointed is one of the most exciting names of Jesus. What a picture of Jesus it has become to frame in my heart! Read the psalmist's words in the margin.

"Thou hast loved righteousness and hated lawlessness;
Therefore God, Thy God, hath anointed Thee
With the oil of gladness above thy companions" (Heb. 1:9).

Anointed is the translation of *Messiah*. *Christ* is the Greek form of the word. We use these names quite frequently.

Another major passage on the Anointed is found in both the Old and New Testaments. The writer of the Book of Hebrews quotes Psalm 45:7. Read Hebrews 1:9 in the margin. The word *Anointed* is used as a verb here, but the concept is the same as in Psalm 2:2.

Recall the meditation process we learned in week 3 and apply it to wearing a name of God.

🌿 **Read Hebrews 1:9 again in the margin on page 70. Let the perimeter of the verse season your understanding of *Anointed*. Read Hebrews 1:1-3 in the margin and write below the characteristics God assigned Jesus.**

• The _____ of all things

• The _____ of God's glory

• The exact _____ of God's nature

• _____ all things by the word of God's power

God, after He spoke long ago to the fathers in the prophets in many portions and in many ways, in these last days has spoken to us in His Son, whom He appointed heir of all things, through whom also He made the world. And He is the radiance of His glory and the exact representation of His nature, and upholds all things by the word of His power (Heb. 1:1-3).

The perimeter of Hebrews 1:9 divulges several photograph-names of Jesus. In ancient times God spoke through His prophets. But now He has spoken through His Son, the heir of all things, the radiance of God's glory, the exact representation of His nature, who upholds all things by the word of God's power.

Refresh your mind's eye with the name *Anointed*. In the Old Testament, anointing was done especially to commission prophets, priests, and kings. Jesus was all three in both His essence and mission. In an anointing ceremony, oil was poured on the head of the person being honored.

🌿 **Write three synonyms for *anointed*.**

_____

_____

Several synonyms are *inaugurated, honored, saturated with, crowned,* and *dedicated.* These words can be used in the next meditation step.

🌿 **Paraphrase Hebrews 1:9.**

_____

_____

I paraphrased the verse by writing, "Jesus loves the good and hates disobedience, so God, His Father, poured out joy on Him more than on anyone who ever lived."

Anointed with Joy

Begin pulverizing Hebrews 1:9 by reading it slowly a few times. Emphasize aloud a different word each time you read the verse. The writer of Hebrews described two major character qualities of the Messiah. Focus on key ideas and words. Ask questions about this name and other key words. For example: What is the balance between being joyful and loving the good and hating disobedience? When did Jesus give evidence of joy? Where does it talk about His companions' not having joy? Why did God choose joy over an anointing of holiness?

The latter part of the verse surprised me. Jesus was anointed with joy. Trying to answer these questions, I saw the Savior as I'd never seen Him. This anointing produced the most joyous, enthusiastic Person who ever lived. Jesus' notable honesty was coated with joy, which helps us understand His attractiveness. Each new day Jesus taught lessons from life or healed someone. I imagine Him captivating inquirers, the needy, and always the crowds. He answered questions with the twelve. What experiences the apostles had following Him!

The Messiah, the Christ, the Anointed who set men free was in their midst. Can't you see Jesus as He belly-laughed with the disciples at some whopper of a fish story or their antics? These men were not the religious dead of Jerusalem's leadership. They were quick to respond, fresh, and free from the trappings of traditionalism and human-made religious laws. With this winsome anointing, Jesus built a team to evangelize a lost world. How did Christ maintain this joy? He was filled with the Spirit and lived only for the glory of His Father.

Jesus' joy was epidemic: "The seventy returned with joy, saying, 'Lord, even the demons are subject to us in Your name' " (Luke 10:17).

Use a concordance and research the word *joy* in the New Testament. Read several passages. Consider memorizing one verse as your "joy verse."

Some cross-references for *joy* in my concordance completed my picture of the Messiah. Hours before He died, Jesus' explained how He had transmitted the overflow of joy to His beloved disciples. Read His words in the margin. Jesus never chose to model the sour face of a discouraged martyr: "Fixing our eyes on Jesus ... who for the joy set before Him endured the cross, despising the shame" (Heb. 12:2).

If the vessel of oil used in anointing someone were large, the olive oil would have flowed from the head, down the beard, and to the shoulders. It may have even trickled down the body, dripping onto the feet.

"These things have I spoken to you, that My joy may be in you, and that your joy may be made full" (John 15:11).

Paul reminded us that Christ is our Head and that we are His body! God could have anointed Jesus with anything. He chose joy! Since believers are the body of Christ, you and I have been splashed with the oil of gladness dripping down from Jesus. His anointing is our anointing. Although joy may be expressed differently through the uniqueness in each of us, His joy is our joy.

🌿 **The next meditation step is to personalize the verse. Write a sentence that personalizes Hebrews 1:9 for you.**

_____

His anointing is our anointing. His joy is our joy.

With all I discovered, I personalized this new insight: "Jesus, You are my joy. I claim Your anointing." During the period when I was understanding this aspect of Jesus, a crisis came in my pastorate. Waiting before God in prayer, I focused on my Savior, the joyous Christ. An immediate, overwhelming joy shot through me, and I laughed in prayer. His anointing of joyous strength was transmitted through me, and God moved victoriously in our church.

How do you keep this anointing of Jesus? Note this surprising cross-reference on joy: "Now may the God of hope fill you with all joy and peace in believing" (Rom. 15:13). This verse says that joy is an attitude that trusts God in every compartment of your life. You have been anointed to bring joy and hope to the death-rattle environment of a lost world. In Christ's anointing there is joy! He is joy, and you echo it! Look at Him daily and think of ways His joy can be expressed through you and passed on to your family, friends, and church.

🌿 **Turn what you've learned into a prayer of praise. Recite Psalm 113:3 from memory. Memorize Isaiah 9:6. Close by praising God for the anointed Christ and the joy He brings to your life.**

Day 4
Everything You'll Ever Need

*T*he prophetic passage Isaiah 9:6 is often quoted when we remember Jesus' birth. However, this verse is great to meditate on all year long, not just at Christmas. It contains four phrases that describe Christ, each illustrating a different promise about God's nature. Let's look at all of them today. At a later time you may want to devote a quiet time to study and meditate on each one.

Write Isaiah 9:6 from memory in the margin.

Wonderful Counselor: Christ Designs Life's Decisions

Life seems so complicated, a maze of endless choices. Buried in Christ, though, are "all the treasures of wisdom and knowledge" (Col. 2:3). During my pastoral ministry I witnessed many astounding victories in those I counseled. Jesus, the Master Counselor, revealed the true problem to us, and the Spirit's conviction brought change. A. W. Tozer explains, "It is change, not time, that turns fools into wise men and sinners into saints."[1]

Jesus wisely responded to pressures and waited for God's best. He spent 40 days in prayer to seek God's counsel for reaching the world. Satan tried to neutralize Jesus' dependence on God with a you-can-have-it-all-now offer. Satan tempted Christ with a crash course on fame! However, Jesus refused this stone-to-bread offer, and "angel-food cake" was on the way! God's will is always "good and acceptable and perfect" (Rom. 12:2).

For a truly changed life, accept no substitutes for meeting with the Wonderful Counselor in His Word. Waiting on God is a supreme mark of discipleship. The Lord will give you either peace where you are or a plan of action. David the shepherd-king said, "My soul, wait in silence for God only" (Ps. 62:5).

What decision are you making now that needs God's advice? Briefly describe it below. Then give it to God in prayer and seek His counsel.

_____

_____

Mighty God: Christ Dominates Life's Demands

The One who created everything visible and invisible certainly has the power to conquer our earth-shattering problems. What was Jesus like, this galactic missionary to earth? Jesus calmed a storm with just two words: " 'Be still' " (Mark 4:39). Empowered by His Father, He stood alone again and again to confront the Pharisees' hypocrisy. Ironically, His supernatural strength was clothed in weakness. Jesus urged us to " 'learn from Me, for I am gentle and humble' " (Matt. 11:29). In the Book of Revelation He is described as both the Lion of Judah and the Lamb of God. He is fierce and authoritative yet vulnerable and pure.

One summer I took the teenagers from my church to a large youth camp in Sebring, Florida. There I witnessed an example of God's strength worked out through a meek response. I'd slept well the night before, but some adults had been kept up by the noise of kids during

Waiting on God is a supreme mark of discipleship.

the wee hours of the morning. At our morning staff meeting a man criticized the pastor of those teens: "We can't keep their attention during the day if we don't sleep at night!" The way he berated my friend Homer, who listened quietly, was embarrassing. Finally, Homer said, "Thank you, Brother, for sharing your feelings." Then another leader broke in to explain: "Many of our teens were burdened for their lost friends at camp. They met for prayer in the chapel. Then some went to wake up their friends. At least 30 youth were saved!" The mighty God working in Homer was so powerful that he didn't have to fight his own battles. His gentleness paved the way for God to get the glory.

"Power is perfected in weakness" (2 Cor. 12:9). King David proclaimed that God's gentleness had made him great (see 2 Sam. 22:36, KJV). Old Testament King Asa knew this principle. Before entering a battle that his army was sure to lose, Asa prayed (in paraphrase): God, Your power is greater than this impossibility. You're carrying us. If we go down, so does Your reputation. Don't let them win (see 2 Chron. 14:11-12; 2 Cor. 12:9). The king leaned totally on Mighty God and won!

What problems in your life need God's mighty hand? Briefly describe one of them below. Then praise God in prayer as the Mighty One who can guide you.

_____

_____

Everlasting Father: Christ Details Life's Dimensions

Your future is fused to the everlasting Father, the Father of eternity. God is bigger than both space and time. Time must constantly be evaluated in light of a timeless eternity: " 'Heaven and earth will pass away, but my words will never pass away' " (Matt. 24:35, NIV).

What we do for Christ can also last forever! In Northfield, Massachusetts, I once sought the hillside grave where D. L. Moody's body is buried. That tombstone symbolizes time laughing at our mortality. I know that Moody isn't there, but he lives in heaven, and his work lives on earth! This 19th-century evangelist preached a simple gospel message that led millions to Jesus. Still going strong are a Bible college, a publishing house, and a radio ministry spawned by his influence.

Because God has set eternity in our hearts, ultimate satisfaction comes only from that which is eternal. Only two things last: God's Word and God's people. Those indwelled by the Father of eternity are time travelers in the truest sense. What eternal potential there is in a life fully surrendered to God!

What eternal potential there is in a life fully surrendered to God!

🍃 **Pray and ask the Father to show you His perspective. Ask yourself,** *What effect will my decisions have on people one hundred years from now?*

God wants you to live with your feet touching time and your heart straining toward His appearing.

🍃 **Is someone you know mourning over the death of a loved one? Why not encourage him or her with the name** *Everlasting Father?*

Prince of Peace: Christ Defuses Life's Disturbances

Wars and rumors of war remind us that no human leader can orchestrate individual or global peace. The Hebrew word for *peace, shalom,* can mean *the possession of adequate resources.* Jesus Himself is adequate! He promises us, " 'My peace I give to you; not as the world gives, do I give to you' " (John 14:27). Unlike the fading banners of protesters crying for peace, Jesus' supply of peace is constant.

Have you ever been in a situation so terrible that you were shattered, speechless? When you don't know what to do or when you're overwhelmed by the situation, turn to Jesus in prayer. Look steadfastly to Him; call out His names. Trusting in Him is the key to inner peace:

> *The steadfast of mind Thou wilt keep in perfect peace,*
> *Because he trusts in Thee (Isa. 26:3).*

🍃 **Recite from memory Isaiah 9:6. Write below the four names that describe Christ:**

W_____ C_____

M_____ G_____

E_____ F_____

P_____ of P_____

🍃 **Close today's lesson by meditating on Isaiah 9:6, using the meditation steps you learned in week 3: perimeter, paraphrase, pulverize, personalize, and pray. Ask God to constantly remind you of these names and what they mean as you live each day for Christ.**

Trusting in Him is the key to inner peace.

---

[1]A. W. Tozer, *That Incredible Christian* (Harrisburg, Penn.: Christian Publications, Inc., 1964), 15.

Day 5
It's All in a Name

*G*od highly exalted Him, and bestowed on Him the name which is above every name" (Phil. 2:9). That name is Jesus. This name is so significant in Scripture that it deserves particular attention. The name *Jesus* is used more than six hundred times in the Gospels. Its Old Testament equivalent is *Joshua*, which means *Jehovah/Yahweh will save* and *God with us.*

The Scriptures teach us that we can do many things in Jesus' name. Read the list in the margin.

The transformation in our lives through His name brings us eternal life. Jesus was called the friend of sinners. Because Jesus chose to identify with sinful people, we are able to be totally changed: "You were washed, ... you were sanctified, ... you were justified in the name of the Lord Jesus" (1 Cor. 6:11). Scripture holds this name in such high regard because of the price God's Son paid to bring about our salvation. At the name of Jesus, one day every person will bow and every tongue will confess Jesus as Lord (see Phil. 2:10-11).

Asking in His Name

The most common way believers use Jesus' name is probably in prayer. People usually take this name for granted when they tag a final "in Jesus name, amen" onto the ends of their prayers, like a religious period at the end of a sentence. What does it mean to ask in Jesus' name?

Let's relate this wonderful name to a staggering promise Jesus gave to His apostles just before His death. Jesus surprised the disciples by telling them that He must go away, but He reassured them that they would see Him again. Then He said, " 'Truly, truly, I say to you, if you shall ask the Father for anything, He will give it to you in My name' " (John 16:23). Jesus repeated it more strongly to make sure the disciples got it: " 'Until now you have asked for nothing in My name; ask, and you will receive, that your joy may be made full' " (John 16:24).

God's power is released when you rightly ask in His name. To ask in Jesus' name means to identify with Christ's will. It is Jesus' "power of attorney" conferred to you to do His business on His behalf. To ask in His name is for Jesus to say the prayer you are praying. It is exactly what Jesus would say if He were bodily present. To use Jesus' name is to bring Him into your circumstance; He is seeing what you see, feeling what you feel, knowing what you know.

Do you pray in Jesus' name? Instead of tagging your prayer with "In Jesus' name, amen," begin your prayers this

In Jesus' name we can—
- **welcome a child** (see Matt. 18:5);
- **gather together** (see Matt. 18:20);
- **perform a miracle** (see Mark 9:39);
- **cast out demons** (see Mark 16:17);
- **proclaim repentance to all nations** (see Luke 24:47);
- **believe** (see John 1:12; 1 John 5:13);
- **ask** (see John 14:13-14; 16:24);
- **call on His name** (see Acts 2:21; Rom. 10:13);
- **be baptized** (see Acts 2:38; 10:48);
- **be saved** (see Acts 4:12);
- **carry His name and suffer for it** (see Acts 9:15-16);
- **risk our lives for His name** (see Acts 15:26);
- **do everything in His name** (see Col. 3:17);
- **confess His name and depart from sin** (see 2 Tim. 2:19);
- **anoint the sick** (see Jas. 5:14).

week with: "Jesus, You are here, so I ask _____ in Your name, invoking Your presence, power, and preeminence in this situation."

To reinforce this wording, fill in the blanks below. Then write it from memory in the margin.

Jesus, You are _____, so I ask _____

in Your _____, invoking Your _____,

_____, and _____

in this _____.

Finally, offer a prayer to Jesus using this wording.

The Significance of "I Am"

The "I am" statements found in John's Gospel both define Jesus' ministry and declare His divinity. Read them in the margin.

The name *Yahweh* was so holy that Jewish people wouldn't even speak it aloud. It is a derivative of the verb *to be, to become.* In John 8:58 Jesus identified Himself with God's revered name: " 'Truly, truly, I say to you, before Abraham was born, I am.' " Just by saying "I am," which comes from the same verb form of *to be,* Jesus was claiming that He is God. The Jewish people understood this reference and considered it blasphemy, punishable by death: "They picked up stones to throw at Him; but Jesus hid Himself" (John 8:59). If God's Son was later put to death for the supposed blasphemy of using these statements, they carry such weight that they are worthy of our careful study.

Choose one of the seven "I am" names of Jesus and relate it to your life by using the meditation steps you learned in week 3: perimeter, paraphrase, pulverize, personalize, and pray.

This week you have considered how you can wear God's names. As you encounter names of God and Jesus in your Bible study, don't pass over them without carefully considering their significance. You might use the names of God as a guide to your daily quiet time with Him. What better way to strengthen your relationship with God than to call Him by His many names and to wear them as you live for Him?

Close this week's study by reciting from memory Psalm 113:3 and Isaiah 9:6.

Jesus' "I Am" Statements
- "I am the bread of life" (see John 6:32-35).
- "I am the light of the world" (see John 8:12).
- "I am the door" (see John 10:7-9).
- "I am the good shepherd" (see John 10:11,14).
- "I am the resurrection and the life" (see John 11:25).
- "I am the way, and the truth, and the life" (see John 14:6).
- "I am the true vine" (see John 15:1,5).

Week 6
Building Bridges to Other Worlds

Day 1
Reaching Difficult People

During my prayer times one summer I felt God prompting me to mow the overgrown yard of our neighbors, a young single mother and her 10-year-old daughter. It wasn't just the foot-high, grassy plains that bothered me. Single-handedly, she was cross-pollinating the neighborhood with her dandelion crop!

We live in Florida, where it doesn't take long for a lush lawn to become a tropical jungle. During the rainy season it's not unusual to mow twice a week. Evidently, the woman didn't own a lawn mower. As if the yard weren't enough, I was also angry because she entertained rowdy guests. She had parties on the weekend, with cars coming and going and friends staying overnight. Our family had tried to be friendly, but our neighbor just didn't want to have anything to do with a preacher's family. We were grateful, though, that her daughter, Jenny, had begun playing with our mentally handicapped son, Paul.

The idea to mow her yard came one morning in my devotions, when the Holy Spirit spoke from Hebrews 10:24, which is printed in the margin. The verse was screaming to be applied. *To stimulate someone to love would be to motivate him or her toward God, who is love,* I thought. *This verse has great potential to be lived.* I paraphrased it to read, "We are to understand each other, asking God to show us how to excite another person toward loving attitudes and actions."

God was asking me to turn my attention toward my neighbor. The Lord had pointed out her obvious need of lawn service. God would use my mowing her lawn as a catalyst to move her toward a loving act and toward Himself.

God's whisper came each time I passed my neighbor's jungle: *Mow that yard.* Excuses came easily. *You've got to be kidding, God!* I thought. *Don't You realize my schedule? Preachers don't mow neighbors' yards.* My seminary hadn't given me a course in "Grass Mowing for Gospel Seed Sowing." Also, in its context Hebrews 10:24 concerns stimulating God's people to good deeds. Furthermore, I rejected the impulse as not being from God. After all, God would have said it specifically: *"Thou shalt take thy lawn mower, go to thy neighbour's yarde, and mow with diligence the grass that is set before thee."*

FOCUS

This week you will learn and apply the Hebrews 10:24 principle for living God's Word.

MEMORY VERSE

Let us consider how to stimulate one another to love and good deeds (Heb. 10:24).

Do not merely listen to the word, and so deceive yourselves. Do what it says (Jas. 1:22, NIV).

A Loving Act

Paul, our mentally handicapped son, enjoyed the healthful exercise and emotional strokes from working outdoors. He became enthusiastic when I finally announced that we were going to mow Jenny's yard. We sneaked over while they were away. Our mower found every rock and stick hiding in the tall brush. Boom! Bang! Paul and I leveled the place. We pushed our lawn mower back home without leaving a calling card.

When our neighbor pulled into her driveway from work, we eagerly peeked out our window to see her reaction. She was astounded. With hands on hips, she walked around the house to survey our work. Then she went door to door, asking several neighbors if they'd mowed her yard. She didn't knock on our door. I guess she didn't expect a pastor to mow an unchurched neighbor's yard.

We mowed her yard two more times. Finally, she came to our door when she returned home. "Reverend Moore, have you been mowing my yard?" she asked. I tried to cushion her embarrassment: "Well, Paul and I have." "Why?" she snapped back. "We're neighbors," I said. "I figured that you didn't have a lawn mower. We just wanted to be neighborly." Her posture softened. "I never had a neighbor do that for me before. Well … thank you. Can I pay you?"

"No thanks, we're neighbors. Let us do it for you," I answered. A month later our neighbor got her own mower, but from that point on we couldn't leave our house without getting a greeting. We had built a bridge to her heart.

Living God's Word

This is an example of what this study is ultimately about—living God's Word. This week we will look at ways to apply what we learn when we spend time growing closer to God.

Briefly describe what it means to live God's Word.

_____

_____

Through the years the Lord has provided multiple opportunities for me to learn the meaning of Hebrews 10:24, which teaches us to serve others and thereby build bridges to their cautious or frigid hearts. Jesus can then walk over those bridges with us. Jesus is the Mediator between this sinful world and a saving God (see 1 Tim. 2:5 in the margin). As Christ's ambassadors we may join Him and serve as a go-between.

Memorize Hebrews 10:24. Then try writing it from memory in the margin.

There is one God, and one mediator also between God and men, the man Christ Jesus (1 Tim. 2:5).

I've read and applied Scripture many times but have not always listened to God each time He's used it to point me toward a specific circumstance. The Lord is serious about those who read or hear Scripture without living it. Read James 1:22 in the margin. Sadly, listening to the Bible without applying it means that we've deceived ourselves.

Do not merely listen to the word, and so deceive yourselves. Do what it says (Jas. 1:22, NIV).

🌿 **List four neighbors who are without Christ. Determine how you can apply Hebrews 10:24 to your relationships with them. Write one idea beside each name.**

Name	Hebrews 10:24 Idea
_____	_____
_____	_____
_____	_____
_____	_____

🌿 **Close today's study by praying for each neighbor.**

Day 2
The Power of Neighboring

One afternoon our attempts to show love to our neighbor suddenly turned sour. Our German shepherd got out of the back yard and bit Jenny, our neighbor's child. Hearing the screams, Clemmie rushed outside. My wife, a pediatrician, quickly assessed the damage: the need for a trip to the emergency room, four or five stitches, and a tetanus shot.

Suddenly, out from Jenny's house came an unhappy aunt whom we'd never met. When Clemmie told her what happened, she announced with anger: "I'm a nurse. I'll take her to the hospital." Clemmie offered, "We'll pay for everything." "You bet you'll pay!" the aunt snapped. She put Jenny into her car and backed it across the street—crunch!—into the side of our station wagon. She drove off without looking back. We prayed hard. Our family had been trying to give a witness to them, and our dog had seemingly destroyed all of our efforts.

When Jenny, her mom, and her aunt returned home, I walked across the street with my checkbook. I apologized in paragraphs: "I'm terribly sorry about the whole thing. We love Jenny. She is a wonderful, caring child. We want to pay for a new dress, the emergency room, and any other medical care."

"No," Jenny's mother said, "you're not going to do it. Jenny probably pushed Paul, and the dog was just defending him. After all, we're neighbors." She used the exact word I'd used about mowing her lawn: *neighbors*. Later, we got to witness about Christ to our neighbor. She didn't come to Christ then, but we built the bridge, and the mother allowed Jenny to go with us to special services at our church. Living God's Word means being a neighbor.

Living God's Word means being a neighbor.

Being a Neighbor

List three persons or families who are close to you.

❏ _____

❏ _____

❏ _____

Check the boxes beside those you would consider your neighbors as illustrated in my example.

Perhaps you've won the right to be called a neighbor. The word *neighbor* means *to draw near.* Maybe you have drawn near to persons in your workplace or have built bridges to a nonbelieving family. You may be the kind of neighbor I would love to have, bringing over a birthday cake or picking up our trash can if dogs knock it over. You already know what it means to be a good neighbor in your community.

These are also good ways to express your Christian faith. Paul said that he went to the trouble of identifying with people "for the sake of the gospel," for the sake of God's good news (1 Cor. 9:23). He also said: "Whether, then, you eat or drink or whatever you do, do all to the glory of God. Give no offense either to Jews or to Greeks or to the church of God; just as I also please all men in all things, not seeking my own profit, but the profit of many, that they may be saved" (1 Cor. 10:31-33). Please whom? Myself? No. "All men."

Serving Others

Paul knew that serving the unsaved is a key to winning them to Christ. In case you or I forget why we're doing it, Paul concentrated on the powerful motivation to serve: "the glory of God." We are called to be true to God. People don't care how much you know until they know how much you care. Then they'll listen. By serving, you gain the right to verbalize your faith. You talk about what Jesus means to you and how your neighbor can know Him, too. Paul witnessed and preached to thousands, but he also knew that the world's route to God had to pass through his own life. People can't deny a life that shows God's love. They sense something supernatural in you when your attitude, your body, and your lips are living God's Word.

Jesus was the greatest bridge builder: from heaven to earth as a lowly, small-town carpenter. He is our ultimate model of neighbor. Read in the margin the way Jesus summarized His earthly ministry. Serving is a wonderful bridge builder, but there is more to living God's Word. Jesus involved Himself in the details of people's lives. Jesus identified with humanity when He "emptied Himself, taking the form of a bond-servant, and being made in the likeness of men" (Phil. 2:7). Like Jesus, we must serve to win hearts and then seek to identify with the lost. The result over time is to be friends with lost persons. Jesus, who pioneered relational evangelism, was criticized for being " 'a friend of tax-gatherers and sinners' " (Matt. 11:19). So must we as we live God's Word.

"The Son of Man did not come to be served, but to serve, and to give His life a ransom for many" (Matt. 20:28).

 Perhaps the Holy Spirit has led you to serve someone and to identify with that person. Now prayerfully seek to share the gospel with him or her. Pray for wisdom and courage to be a neighbor to others.

 Close today's study by meditating on Hebrews 10:24.

Day 3
Finding Common Ground

The ultimate way to live God's Word is to treat the world as your neighborhood. What do you have in common with your neighbors? You share bordering property—whether land or apartment walls. Your kids ride bikes together. You vote in the same precinct. Similarly, you can find common ground with almost everyone you encounter. In a classic passage of Scripture, 1 Corinthians 9:19-23, the apostle Paul detailed this approach of finding something in common with nonbelievers. This passage explains how to build bridges to hard hearts.

Building Bridges

 Read 1 Corinthians 9:19-23 in your Bible. Write in the margin a paraphrase of the passage.

Circle key words in your paraphrase on page 83. Refer to your paraphrase throughout today's study.

Paul said, "Though I am free from all men, I have made myself a slave to all, that I might win the more" (1 Cor. 9:19). Technically, Paul was free, but he chose to make himself the servant of others to win them. Following Jesus' example, Paul became a bridge. He "crossed over boundaries of prejudice in race and religion to win men and women for Jesus Christ."[1] Later he no longer had to make himself serve. God brought about a change in this tough guy, so that he served spontaneously: "I have become all things to all men, that I may by all means save some" (1 Cor. 9:22). Paul was living God's Word!

Does this mean that Paul went around like a mom, picking up for people? Was he like a self-appointed waiter? The image is broader than that and more difficult. His passion was clear: to win the largest possible number of people to Christ. The word *win* (*gain* in the *King James Version*) is used five times in verses 19-22. It means *to possess, acquire* for Christ. Paul's plan was to do whatever it took to bring people to Jesus. He became their "slave" so that they could know Christ's freedom from hell. Let's look at four groups Paul worked to convert and draw correlations with people you and I meet.

The Jews. "To the Jews I became as a Jew, that I might win Jews" (1 Cor. 9:20). Relating to Jews shouldn't have been difficult for Paul, who had been reared in a Jewish family. Paul used instance after instance in Acts to refer to Old Testament teachings, Jewish ceremonies, laws, and the hope of the Messiah. To our churched but lost culture we witness to a living Christ, our Savior from sin, who is Lord over all (see Luke 6:46-49).

Those under the law. To those who were under the law, Paul made it a point to empathize with their lifestyle (see 1 Cor. 9:20b). Paul had been schooled in the top seminary for strict rabbis. Also, he had once been part of the orthodox branch of Judaism, the Pharisees. Although Paul was no longer bound by the law, he chose not to offend so that he could win the right to witness. Like Paul, we are to be sensitive to those who have different convictions. We must identify with others as we seek to get close enough to share the gospel.

Those under no law. Paul was no stranger to those who were not Jews: the Gentiles. Most of them used Greek or Roman Latin for business. Paul had been reared in the seaport city of Tarsus, where he had learned Greek. To those who weren't reared with God's law, Paul started with the basics. He taught about the Creator from heaven who gives us rain (see Acts 14:17). He taught that God is not an image but alive. Then Paul witnessed of Christ. He became a Gentile to the Gentiles. Paul described this group: "To those not having the law I became like one not having the law (though I am not free from God's law but am under Christ's

> Paul's plan was to do whatever it took to bring people to Jesus.

law), so as to win those not having the law" (1 Cor. 9:21, NIV). He was under the law of Christ and did not compromise his walk. Still, he reaped a continual harvest of souls.

We are to take Christ to people in a lost world rather than count on their joining us at church on Sunday. It has been a joy to witness and win people to Christ in unusual places. For example, our family was camped in the Smokies at 10,000 feet, which was above the cloud line. Because of fog the forest ranger wouldn't allow anyone to drive downhill that Sunday morning. This was God's timing for us to talk about Christ with fellow campers. Our three kids distributed hand-printed invitations to an informal church service at the campground's outdoor amphitheater. Each family member had a part in the worship service, and about six families attended whom we had not met before. This occasion was a testimony to our family's living God's Word.

The weak. Paul also identified with those who were superspiritual: "To the weak I became weak, that I might win the weak" (1 Cor. 9:22). Though they weren't saved, they were still "overscrupulous" (1 Cor. 9:22, Williams). They had lots of rules to keep and wanted you to keep them, too.

Sometimes we can serve and win to Christ not only the spiritually weak but also the physically weak. When our son Paul was born, I got to know Jim, a first-time dad, in the waiting room. When both of our babies were born, I visited Jim and Virginia down the hall and had prayer with them for their new son. They lived within blocks of our church, so we visited them at home. We discovered that they had financial needs. For weeks we shared with them food that the church had brought us. This built a strong bridge, and both of our new friends received Christ, were baptized, and grew.

As you grow in your relationship with God, He will give you His eyes to see the unreleased potential in people you meet who are waiting to be loved and encouraged.

 Think of someone you know at work or in your neighborhood who is facing a crisis or has a need. Write his or her name here: _____

Pray for this person. During your quiet times this week, ask God to show you ways to encourage and lift the person. Then follow God's guidance as you serve this person.

 Memorize James 1:22 to close today's study.

> **As you grow in your relationship with God, He will give you His eyes to see the unreleased potential in people you meet who are waiting to be loved and encouraged.**

[1]Alan Redpath, *The Royal Route to Heaven: Studies in First Corinthians* (Westwood, N.J.: Fleming H. Revell Co., 1960), 110.

Day 4
Sharing the Gospel with Everyone

A concrete contractor lived in our neighborhood. When we needed a new building at our church, I persuaded him to bid on the contract. His company got it, so we had something to talk about. His wife opened a ceramics workshop and kiln in an add-on room in their home. I had made pottery in the past, so I occasionally talked with her about our common interest.

God finally opened a door through a child. Michael was their eight-year-old, who played with our son Bruce. I had taught Bruce to use the Wordless Book Gospel tool. One day he led Michael to Christ. The parents called me up and wanted to talk. After an hour of witnessing, both the husband and the wife prayed to receive Christ, and I soon baptized all three. Then things mushroomed. This couple witnessed to their grown sons, and the sons and their wives were saved. Only the Lord could have placed us with such special new friends on a strategic block.

Repeat from memory James 1:22 and meditate on it, using the meditation steps you learned in week 3.

Be Ready to Share

Our lives should open the door for verbally and repeatedly sharing the gospel as we live God's Word. Let's be absolutely clear about the meaning of the familiar word *gospel*.

What does *gospel* mean? Check one.
❑ **truth**
❑ **a religious song**
❑ **good news of Christ**
❑ **plan of salvation**

A veteran missionary challenged me to give him the gospel. When I quoted some verses, he responded with a story: "A car overturns, and someone is crushed inside. He's dying. You have five minutes to win him to Christ. What would you say?" Then he showed me a summary passage that greatly increased my witnessing effectiveness, 1 Corinthians 15:1-4. These verses give God's definition of the gospel, the good news of Christ.

Read 1 Corinthians 15:1-4 in the margin. Fill in the missing words in the four crucial points of the gospel.
• **We witness of _____. We share who Christ is: the Anointed One, Messiah, God's Son, God Himself.**

Now I make known to you, brethren, the gospel which I preached to you, which also you received, in which also you stand, by which also you are saved, if you hold fast the word which I preached to you, unless you believed in vain. For I delivered to you as of first importance what I also received, that Christ died for our sins according to the Scriptures, and that He was buried, and that He was raised on the third day according to the Scriptures (1 Cor. 15:1-4).

- Christ died for our _____. He didn't just die; everyone does that. Christ died as a substitute for our sins. Jesus became our sin bearer; He became sin for us (also see 2 Cor. 5:21).
- Christ was _____. He experienced the full torture of death by asphyxiation and exposure as he hung on the cross. Jesus' loved ones sealed His body in a tomb for three days, where He had no water or fresh air. He had truly died on that cross.
- Christ was _____ on the third day. Jesus rose again. He came back alive in bodily form and was seen for 40 days. Jesus was also seen by five hundred people at once as He ascended. (When I witness, I usually ask the person to receive Christ at this point.)

In summary, the gospel (good news) is: (1) Christ (2) died for our sins, (3) was buried, and (4) was raised to life. Be clear in your gospel presentation, and the Holy Spirit will make your witnessing His witnessing.

Reaching Your World

We live in seven worlds or communities where we can witness and have an influence for Christ. These seven worlds are pictured in the diagram on page 88. They are the worlds of our home, our neighborhood, and our workplace or school. There is another world of social relationships—people in clubs or organizations we belong to. Don't overlook church relationships. I've discovered that many husbands and grown children of active members regularly come to church but are lost. We also have tremendous opportunities to witness through our hobbies and other recreational activities.

Last, in the lost world more than one billion people have never heard the gospel and have never had a Christmas or an Easter. A billion more have never met a believer or have never been inside an evangelistic church. Pray for unreached people groups, nations, and missionaries. To live God's Word is to penetrate our seven worlds with the gospel, His love, and good works.

Write an unsaved person's name beside each of the seven worlds in the diagram on page 88. Pray for each person you listed.

When was the last time you shared the gospel? Keep praying for your neighbors who need Christ. Write their names in the margin.

To live God's Word is to penetrate our seven worlds with the gospel, His love, and good works.

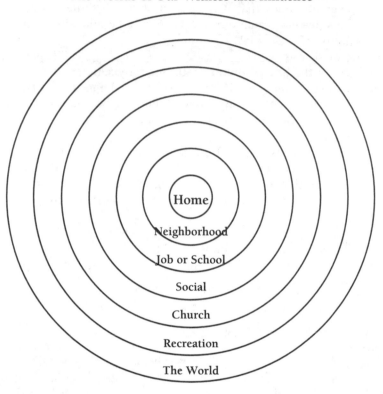

The Worlds of Our Witness and Influence

- Home
- Neighborhood
- Job or School
- Social
- Church
- Recreation
- The World

Commit to learn a witnessing method this year. Your church may have one or more it teaches regularly. Go and tell someone the gospel. Add these important evangelism verses to ones you already know: Romans 3:23; 5:8; 6:23; Hebrews 9:27-28; 1 Corinthians 15:3-4; Ephesians 2:8-9; John 1:12; 5:24; Revelation 3:20. Memorize them over the next several weeks.

Day 5
Strengthening the Bridge

Your neighborhood, office, or club is just as strategic as mine is. God has a plan for you there, and He will give you creative ideas for crossing the bridge to hundreds of hearts—nonbelievers or Christians. Let's look at six practical ways to apply the Hebrews 10:24 principle for living God's Word.

The Hebrews 10:24 Principle

Hebrews 10:24, which you will apply in today's lesson, is one of your memory verses for this week. Write this verse from memory in the margin.

As you read each of the following suggestions, think of someone you might minister to by using that particular tool. You will be asked at the end of the day to list his or her name and to identify the tool.

Grace words. Minister grace to people with your words. You can probably recall words people have said about you. Some words stick for a lifetime. Words have life-changing power. In Ephesians 4:29 God gives us a surprising opportunity. Read Paul's words in the margin.

God's grace is priceless. Yet He has trusted you with the ministry of speaking words that give grace—words that build up and lift spirits and change lives. Grace is instantly channeled into the hearts of others through your tongue. Read Proverbs 16:24 in the margin.

God has taught me to pass on a verse of Scripture to encourage and bless someone in Christ. I pray, using the right verse from those I've memorized, a verse God has used in my life. People respond wonderfully to Deuteronomy 1:11. Other verses that encourage others are Ecclesiastes 3:14; Isaiah 49:15-16; 63:9; and Jeremiah 31:3.

Letters. Write encouraging notes and letters to people. Your letters will be kept, possibly outliving your earthly walk by decades. Read Proverbs 25:25 in the margin.

Thank-you letters have become rare today. People offer a quick thanks for a gift you spent three hours shopping for. Write to a lonely widow, a hurting teen, a thoughtful neighbor, or a person in prison. To feel a closer bond with a congregation I pastored, I began sending a birthday card to every member. As a result, I got more words of thanks and hugs than all of the compliments on my sermons in a year!

I have a sister who wouldn't communicate with me at one point because of her spiritual condition. My wife and I were praying about her when Clemmie said: "It's nearly Valentine's Day. Send her a card." On Valentine's Day I got a telephone call from my sister. She was very emotional, saying that I was the only person who had remembered her. She asked forgiveness for her negative attitude. With that card came a renewed relationship. And in a few months she gave her life to Christ!

Listening. By listening, we show our consideration and sometimes discover the unmarked route to a needy heart. I recall asking a simple question to a church member who had called me on the phone. She answered in a 40-minute torrent of words—hurts, anger, and needs. On another occasion my wife overheard me giving advice to a pastor over

Let no unwholesome word proceed from your mouth, but only such a word as is good for edification according to the need of the moment, that it may give grace to those who hear (Eph. 4:29).

Pleasant words are a honeycomb, Sweet to the soul and healing to the bones (Prov. 16:24).

Like cold water to a weary soul, So is good news from a distant land (Prov. 25:25).

the phone. Grabbing a pencil, she wrote, "Just listen to him." Her counsel was right on target.

Touch. Touching others can also communicate care and love. I've learned over a hard 40 years that God wants to hug people through me. Some men find it difficult to hug, hold, or play with their own children. Sometimes it's because their fathers never hugged them.

Jesus, on the other hand, touched the dead, the sick, the leper, the unclean. Miracles happened. As a man's understanding of God's unlimited love grows, so can his desire to touch the hurting. He might hold a handshake for a moment of prayer between men. With pats on the back or an occasional bear hug, a man can draw nearer to a guy in need.

Hospitality. Use holidays and special days as times to invite neighbors to your home. Give a birthday party for your child's friend. The parents will be delighted. Or have an open house and let your children deliver invitations. We did this at Christmas and had people we'd never known sitting in our living room eating fruitcake. They listened to our kids sing a carol and to little Martha quote the Christmas account from Luke 2.

Prayer. Praying together is a strong means of encouraging people to love. You have a great opportunity to pray both for and with a nonbeliever when you have him over for dinner. If you pray for that person in his presence, it makes God seem more real. Also, as people hear how you get answers to prayer, they may ask you to pray for their needs. Keep alert. Crises will come to families around you. In times of sickness, accidents, death, and job loss, an act of love will link your heart with theirs and will open the door for you to invite them to your church.

An act of love will link your heart with theirs.

Unleash the Hebrews 10:24 principle. This is one verse of thousands that scream to be applied in life. Write the names of six persons in your world who need a word from God. Pray about them and do what God directs. Write one of the six tools you studied today after each name.

Name	Tool
_____	_____
_____	_____
_____	_____
_____	_____
_____	_____
_____	_____

The Holy Spirit will teach you how to "stimulate ... to love and good deeds" (Heb. 10:24). And the next time your neighbor neglects his lawn for a few weeks, well ...

Live God's Word

You have completed *Living God's Word,* but you have only begun to live God's Word. You have been introduced to new tools to help you grow in your relationship with God. Now it's up to you! It will take you from six to eight weeks to master these disciplines. Use the suggestions in the margin to maintain your regular quiet time and to study, memorize, and meditate on God's Word. Let God's Word become a part of who you are and how you live. Reach out and serve others as you learn and live God's Word.

Reflect on your study of *Living God's Word* and complete the following statements.

The most important truth I learned for my spiritual

life was _____

The Scripture passage I memorized that spoke to me with

the most meaning was _____

Write it below from memory.

_____

_____

_____

One important change the Lord and I need to make in my

life is _____

_____

The next step I need to take is _____

_____

Close your study with prayer. Make a commitment to God to grow in your relationship with Him.

Master the Disciplines

- **Be accountable to a friend about your quiet time.**
- **Using your weekly Sunday School Bible passage, look for something to know, stop, change, or start.**
- **Memorize and meditate on two key verses each week from John's Gospel.**
- **Use the ideas in the activity on page 56 to visualize a Scripture passage.**
- **Meditate on the "I Am" names of Jesus (see p. 78).**
- **Memorize verses on witnessing.**
- **Prayerfully choose one person to whom you will teach the disciplines you have learned.**

Leader Guide

Use this section to guide your group study. Optimal group size is from 10 to 12 persons. Recommended time segments provide for one-hour sessions. Do not let this guide restrict you. Freely follow the Holy Spirit's leadership. Distribute workbooks at least one week in advance or conduct a brief introductory session to overview the study and to distribute workbooks. Group session 1 should follow members' completion of week 1 in this workbook.

Session 1

Welcome to the Banquet

Review Time (5 minutes)
Introduce yourself and allow members to do so. Quote the memory verse, Jeremiah 15:16. Ask volunteers to say it from different translations and to share what God said to them through the verse.

Sharing Time (45 minutes)
1. Ask, Over the past week which Scriptures from your personal Bible study, a sermon, or a lesson challenged you to repentance, renewal, or new habits? Allow several members to share.
2. Focus on the activity in which members applied the know-stop-change-start process to Romans 13:8-14. Let several identify what God told them they should know, stop, change, or start. Ask, What specifically will you do in response to God?
3. Say, You may be missing God's Word because you are picking the wrong packages, settling for substitutes, or evading the unfamiliar. Based on day 2's lesson, discuss what these phrases mean and how each barrier can be overcome.
4. Ask: Which did you identify as an area on which you need to focus in your spiritual growth: daily time with God, God's direction through other people, or Christian biography? What one action will you take this week to develop a healthy appetite for God's Word? Ask members to share.
5. Discuss the questions we can ask about a Scripture to fully experience God's Word:
   • What does the passage say?
   • Why was the passage written?
   • How am I to experience the passage now?
   Ask: Did you find these questions helpful? Why or why not? Have you been asking these? Will you in the future?
6. Say: This week you have discovered the value of assimilating Scripture into your life. You have begun to develop tools for applying God's truths. The weeks that follow will build on this material as you learn how to apply God's Word in your daily life. Encourage members to keep a journal during this study to record assignments that may require extra space.

Prayer Time (10 minutes)
Explain that because this study progressively leads participants to develop skills in studying and applying God's Word, completing the daily activities in this book before each group session is very important.

Ask members to share prayer concerns about their expectations for this study. Write expectations on a sheet of paper; members will reflect on these in group session 6. Pray for each concern. Close by praying that members will hear and understand what God says to them through their study of His Word and that they will be committed to obeying Him.

Before members leave, ask each to choose a partner. Ask partners to contact each other during the week to learn whether they are completing their daily work and are keeping their commitments to study and apply God's Word.

Session 2

The Surprising Habit That Changes Your Life

Review Time (5 minutes)
Divide into pairs and review this week's memory verses, Philippians 4:13 and John 16:24. Ask

members to share what God has been saying to them about Scripture memorization through these verses.

Sharing Time (45 minutes)

1. Review the five reasons Scripture memorization is valuable. Write these on a poster or chalkboard as you list each one. Highlight material from throughout the week's lessons as needed. Ask members to testify to the validity of each reason:
   • Handling pressure
   • Getting guidance
   • Gaining victory over sin
   • Making witnessing and discipleship simple
   • Receiving answers to prayers
2. Ask: What is your attitude toward memorizing Scripture? How has it changed this week?
3. Review the process of Scripture memorization:
   Step 1: Begin with a positive attitude.
   Step 2: Glue the reference to the first words.
   Step 3: Memorize bite by bite.
   Step 4: Review, review, review.
   Step 5: Meditate on the verse(s).
   Step 6: Use spare time wisely.
   Step 7: Team with a friend.
   Step 8: Use a Scripture-memorization system.
4. Practice steps 2, 3, and 4 of this process with the group, using 1 Peter 5:7. Point out that this is one of next week's memory verses.
5. Discuss using spare time wisely. Ask members to brainstorm places and times in their daily schedules suitable for learning and reviewing Scripture.
6. Ask accountability partners to check each other's Scripture memorization during each week.
7. Ask, Do you have a plan for Scripture memorization? Encourage several members to share plans.

Prayer Time (10 minutes)

Say, This week we learned that God has certain guidelines for answered prayer:
   • Ask with sins confessed.
   • Ask by faith.
   • Ask in Jesus' name.
   • Ask according to His will.
   Divide into groups of four. Say: Share in your group which of these areas needs strengthening in your life. Spend the remainder of the time praying for one another that each of you might grow in your prayer life.

Session 3

An Unexpected Source of Success

Review Time (5 minutes)

Say: Beginning with this week's verses, review with a partner all of your memory verses: 1 Peter 5:7, Psalm 1:2-3, Jeremiah 15:16, Philippians 4:13, and John 16:24. Choose someone you have not paired with before.

Sharing Time (45 minutes)

1. Ask, What is meditation? Allow several members to give their definitions. Summarize the discussion by saying, Meditation is reflective thinking with a view to living God's will as revealed in Scripture.
2. Say, For some of us, the idea of meditating on Scripture may be new. Ask, Is that the case for anyone in our group? Encourage several members to share their preconceptions and experiences with meditation prior to this study.
3. Ask members to name five meditation steps they learned this week. As each step is named, write the significant *p* word on a poster or chalkboard:
   Step 1: Understand the perimeter of the verse.
   Step 2: Paraphrase the verse.
   Step 3: Pulverize the verse.
   Step 4: Personalize the verse.
   Step 5: Pray the verse into your life.
   Briefly discuss each step. Ask, Which step or steps challenge you most?
4. Divide the group in half and assign a facilitator for each group. Ask the two groups to practice the meditation steps, using Psalm 1:2-3 or a passage of your choice. Allow the groups to work for 20 minutes. Call them back together to report.

Prayer Time (10 minutes)

Conduct a group prayer time. Encourage members to pray aloud for specific needs and concerns that surfaced during today's group session. Close by asking God to guide members as they practice meditation as a tool for living God's Word.

Session 4

The Time of Your Life

Review Time (5 minutes)
Ask pairs to review this week's memory verses, John 4:23 and Psalm 143:8. Ask, What did God say to you this week through these two verses?

Sharing Time (40 minutes)
1. Ask: Before this week's study, what was your quiet time like with God? Was it daily? Was it weekly or weakly? Did you have a plan? In other words, was it regular and satisfying to your spiritual growth? Allow several members to share what their private times with God were like entering this week's study. Keep the focus on the past at this point.
2. Ask, Why is it important to spend time alone with God? Three reasons were introduced this week.
   • Have fellowship with the Father.
   • Prepare for the day.
   • God shapes your life.
   Ask: Which of these—or another reason you thought of during your study—is most important to you? Why? Allow several members to answer.
3. Say, Spending time with God yields rewards:
   Reward 1: Reaping a life for God
   Reward 2: Knowing and loving God
   Reward 3: Becoming like Christ
   Reward 4: Being empowered for daily living
   Briefly review these with the group. Encourage testimonies by members.
4. Say: This week we considered ideas on how to spend time alone with God. Let's review each area. Divide into three groups. Either write the assignments on cards and give them to the facilitators of the small groups or lead the entire group yourself.
   • A place for time with God. Ask, Where do you meet with God? Describe it to the group.
   • A time to meet with God. Ask: When do you

meet with God? Is this a new time you began this week or one you have maintained for some time? Why is this a good time for you?
   • A plan for time with God. What plan do you use when you meet with God? Briefly describe it.
   End the discussion time by asking, As you studied these suggestions, which area did you identify as needing work to strengthen your quiet time?

Prayer Time (15 minutes)
Say: Two days of our study this week were devoted to prayer. We considered two principles of prayer:
   Principle 1: We limit God when we don't pray.
   Principle 2: God is able and ready, waiting for us to believe Him.
Both principles are linked with acting on God's promises as given in Scripture. Ask: What has God said to you this week about your prayer life? What concerns about your prayer life will you allow us to join you in working on? Close with prayer for the concerns mentioned. Thank God for prayer and His eagerness to hear from His children.

Session 5

Wearing God's Names

Review Time (5 minutes)
Remind members that this week's study focused on the importance of names that identify and describe the Deity. Ask two members to recite the two memory verses for the week, Psalm 113:3 and Isaiah 9:6.

Sharing Time (45 minutes)
1. Say, Tell the group your full name and what it means. Ask each member to share his or her name and its meaning.
2. Ask members to respond to the statement "Your capacity to trust the Lord is linked to a knowledge of His names and character" (p. 67).
3. Ask, How does the title *Carpenter* bring meaning to your relationship with Christ? Allow members to share their thoughts from day 2.
4. Recite Psalm 113:3. Discuss the importance of

praising God's name. Ask each member to give a name, title, or phrase that praises God's name.

5. Recite Isaiah 9:6. Divide into four groups. Assign each group one of the names found in Isaiah 9:6: Wonderful Counselor, Mighty God, Everlasting Father, or Prince of Peace. Instruct each group to determine how a person can wear this name of Jesus in daily living. Give the groups 15 minutes to work. Then call them back together to report.

Prayer Time (10 minutes)
Say: Probably, the most common way we use Jesus' name is in prayer. We will close by praying in Jesus' name. Encourage everyone to participate. Instruct members to pray, using the following format.

Jesus, You are here, so I ask _____ in Your name, invoking Your presence, power, and preeminence in this situation.

Session 6

Building Bridges to Other Worlds

Review Time (5 minutes)
Divide members into pairs and ask them to review the memory verses for the past six weeks. Ask members to share what God has said to them through these memory verses.

Sharing Time (40 minutes)
1. Ask, What does the word *neighbor* mean? (*draw near*) Instruct the group to name characteristics of a good neighbor. Write these on a poster or chalkboard. After the list is complete, say, Examine our list and mentally check the characteristics that are true of you. Ask as a thought question, Do you consider yourself a good neighbor?
2. Ask, What primary characteristic of being a neighbor did Jesus portray? Listen to Matthew 20:28: " 'The Son of Man did not come to be served, but to serve, and to give His life a ransom for many.' " Circle or add *servant* to the list of characteristics.
3. Recite Hebrews 10:24. Say, This week we considered ways to build bridges to other worlds by

applying the Hebrews 10:24 principle for living God's Word. Ask, What do we mean by "other worlds"? Allow several members to respond. Refer to the illustration on page 88.
4. Recite James 1:22. Ask, What does it mean to live God's Word? Encourage all members to answer.
5. Say, Part of living God's Word is sharing the gospel with those in our worlds. Ask pairs to discuss their plans for sharing the gospel this week.
6. Review the six suggestions for applying the Hebrews 10:24 principle for living God's Word:
   - grace words
   - letters
   - listening
   - touch
   - hospitality
   - prayer

Encourage testimonies by members who have implemented one or more of these suggestions.

Prayer Time (5 minutes)
Ask members to pair with their accountability partners. Instruct them to pray by name for each other to live God's Word in their worlds.

Reflection and Commitment Time (10 minutes)
1. Allow members to share what God has done during the past six weeks. Refer to the list of expectations members compiled during group session 1.
2. Ask, What do you sense that God wants you to do next to continue growing? Discuss the suggestions in the margin on page 91.
3. Ask, What can we do as a group to support one another? Consider these suggestions:
   - Continue meeting regularly as a group for encouragement and prayer.
   - Study *When God Speaks, In God's Presence, The Kingdom Agenda,* or *How to Study Your Bible.**
4. Recommend that after members have mastered the skills in *Living God's Word,* they use *Day by Day in God's Kingdom: A Discipleship Journal** during their quiet times. It provides prayer lists and 13 weeks of Scriptures and discipleship activities.

*These resources may be purchased by contacting the Customer Service Center; 127 Ninth Avenue, North; Nashville, TN 37234-0113; by faxing (615) 251-5933; by emailing *customerservice@lifeway.com*; by ordering online at *www.lifeway.com*; by calling 1-800-458-2772; or by visiting a Lifeway Christian Store.

Living God's Word

CHRISTIAN GROWTH STUDY PLAN
Preparing Christians to Serve

In the Christian Growth Study Plan (formerly the Church Study Course) this book, *Living God's Word: Practical Lessons for Applying Scripture to Life,* is a resource for course credit in the subject area Ministry in the Christian Growth category of diploma plans. To receive credit, read the book; complete the learning activities; attend group sessions; show your work to your pastor, a staff member, or a church leader; then complete the following information. This form may be duplicated. Send the completed page to:

Christian Growth Study Plan, MSN 117
127 Ninth Avenue, North
Nashville, TN 37234-0117
Fax: (615) 251-5067

For information about the Christian Growth Study Plan, refer to the current *Christian Growth Study Plan Catalog.* Your church office may have a copy. If not, request a free copy from the Christian Growth Study Plan office, (615) 251-2525.

Living God's Word: Practical Lessons for Applying Scripture to Life
COURSE NUMBER CG-0224

PARTICIPANT INFORMATION

Social Security Number | Personal CGSP Number* | Date of Birth

Name (First, MI, Last) | Home Phone
☐ Mr. ☐ Miss
☐ Mrs. ☐

Address (Street, Route, or P.O. Box) | City, State | Zip Code

CHURCH INFORMATION

Church Name

Address (Street, Route, or P. O. Box) | City, State | Zip Code

CHANGE REQUEST ONLY

☐ Former Name

☐ Former Address | City, State | Zip Code

☐ Former Church | Zip Code

Signature of Pastor, Conference Leader, or Other Church Leader | Date

*New participants are requested but not required to give SS# and date of birth. Existing participants, please give CGSP# when using SS# for the first time. Thereafter, only one ID# is required. Mail to: Christian Growth Study Plan, 127 Ninth Ave., North, MSN 117, Nashville, TN 37234-0117. Fax: (615)251-5067